The American Revolution

Allen C. Guelzo, Ph.D.

THE
GREAT
COURSES®

PUBLISHED BY:

THE GREAT COURSES
Corporate Headquarters
4840 Westfields Boulevard, Suite 500
Chantilly, Virginia 20151-2299
Phone: 1-800-832-2412
Fax: 703-378-3819
www.thegreatcourses.com

Allen C. Guelzo, Ph.D.

Henry R. Luce Professor of the Civil War Era,
Director of Civil War Era Studies, and Associate Director
of the Civil War Institute, Gettysburg College

Dr. Allen C. Guelzo is the Henry R. Luce Professor of the Civil War Era, the director of Civil War Era Studies, and associate director of the Civil War Institute at Gettysburg College in Gettysburg, Pennsylvania. He was born in Yokohama, Japan, but grew up in Springfield, Pennsylvania. He holds an M.A. and a Ph.D. in History from the University of Pennsylvania, where he wrote his dissertation under the direction of Bruce Kuklick, Alan C. Kors, and Richard S. Dunn. Dr. Guelzo previously taught at both Drexel University and Eastern University in St. Davids, Pennsylvania. At Eastern University, where he taught for 13 years, he was the Grace Ferguson Kea Professor of American History and, from 1998 to 2004, the founding dean of the Templeton Honors College.

Dr. Guelzo is the author of numerous books on American intellectual history and on Abraham Lincoln and the Civil War era, beginning with his first work, *Edwards on the Will: A Century of American Theological Debate* (Wesleyan University Press, 1989). His second book, *For the Union of Evangelical Christendom: The Irony of the Reformed Episcopalians* (Pennsylvania State University Press, 1994), won the Albert C. Outler Prize for Ecumenical Church History of the American Society of Church History. He wrote *The Crisis of the American Republic: A History of the Civil War and Reconstruction Era* for the St. Martin's Press American History series in 1995 and followed that with a new edition of Josiah G. Holland's 1866 biography, *Life of Abraham Lincoln*, in 1998 for the Bison Books series of classic Lincoln biography reprints from the University of Nebraska Press.

Dr. Guelzo's book *Abraham Lincoln: Redeemer President* (William B. Eerdmans Press, 1999) won both the Lincoln Prize and the Abraham Lincoln Institute Prize in 2000. In 2003, his article "Defending Emancipation: Abraham Lincoln and the Conkling Letter, 1863" won *Civil War History*'s John T. Hubbell Prize for the best article of that year. Dr. Guelzo's book *Lincoln's Emancipation Proclamation: The End of Slavery in America* (Simon & Schuster, 2004) also won the Lincoln Institute Prize and the Lincoln Prize for 2005, making him the first double Lincoln laureate in the history of both prizes. His article "Houses Divided: Lincoln, Douglas, and the Political Landscape of Illinois, 1858" was featured in the September 2007 issue of *The Journal of American History*. His book on the Lincoln-Douglas debates of 1858, *Lincoln and Douglas: The Debates that Defined America*, was published by Simon & Schuster in 2008.

Dr. Guelzo has written for *The Washington Post*, the *Los Angeles Times*, *The Wall Street Journal*, *First Things*, the *Claremont Review of Books*, and *Books and Culture* and has been featured on NPR's *Weekend Edition Sunday* and Brian Lamb's *Booknotes*. He is a member of the board of directors of the Abraham Lincoln Association, the Abraham Lincoln Institute, and the Historical Society of the Episcopal Church; a member of the advisory councils of the Abraham Lincoln Bicentennial Commission; a research associate for the McNeil Center for Early American Studies at the University of Pennsylvania; and a member of the American Historical Association, the Organization of American Historians, the Society for Historians of the Early American Republic, the Society of Civil War Historians, and the Union League of Philadelphia.

Dr. Guelzo has been a fellow of the American Council of Learned Societies (1991–1992), the McNeil Center for Early American Studies (1992–1993), the Charles Warren Center for American Studies at Harvard University (1994–1995), and the James Madison Program in American Ideals and Institutions at Princeton University (2002–2003).

Among his other honors, Dr. Guelzo has earned the Lincoln Award of the Lincoln Group of the District of Columbia, the Lincoln Medal of the Union League Club of New York City, and the Medal of Honor of the Daughters of the American Revolution. In 2005, he was nominated by President George W. Bush and confirmed by the Senate as a member of the National Council on the Humanities.

Professor Guelzo's other Teaching Company courses include *The American Mind*; *Mr. Lincoln: The Life of Abraham Lincoln*; and *History of the United States, 2ⁿᵈ Edition*, which he team-taught with Professor Patrick N. Allitt and Professor Gary W. Gallagher.

Dr. Guelzo lives in Paoli and Gettysburg, Pennsylvania, with his wife, Debra.

Table of Contents
The American Revolution

Table of Contents
The American Revolution

The American Revolution

Scope:

This Teaching Company course is devoted to a survey of the American Revolution, from its outbreak at Lexington and Concord in April, 1775, until its close with the signing of the Treaty of Paris in 1783 and the dispersion of the American Continental army. It is a story concerned mostly with a war—an 18th-century war in particular—which requires some understanding of what the nature of 18th-century warfare was and how it shaped the American Revolution for both American and British soldiers. This course begins with a very short overview of the issues that brought the North American British colonies into conflict with the British Empire, and moves from there at once to the outbreak of hostilities between American and British forces. The 24 lectures in this series are built around three important questions:

1. What were the armies and navies which fought the Revolution like? How different was the British regular from the American militiaman and Continental regular? What was combat in the 18th century like?

2. What were the major campaigns of the Revolution? How important were Trenton, Saratoga, and Yorktown? What difference did the formal intervention of the French in 1778 make?

3. Who were the leaders of the Revolution? In particular, how much of a difference was made by the military leadership on both sides—by George Washington, Nathaniel Greene, Lord George Germain, Sir William Howe, and even King George III?

We will take the road to Revolution in the first three lectures by examining the political conflict that originated over imperial policy-making in 1763 and include a survey of the chief enforcers of that policy, the British army in North America. In Lecture Four, we stop for a close look at the British army—its men, tactics, and weaponry. Then, in Lectures Five through Twelve, I will introduce the first campaigns of the war—the organization of a Continental army under George Washington, the abandonment of Boston by the British, the ill-fated American invasion of Canada, the British capture of New York, and the miraculous rallying of American fortunes at Trenton and Princeton. Lecture Thirteen will shift attention to the Continental Congress—or rather, the ways in which the Congress failed to support its own army. Lectures Fourteen through Seventeen return us to the fighting, this time covering the second phase of the war with Gen. John Burgoyne's doomed expedition to Albany, Sir William Howe's brilliant but feckless capture of Philadelphia, and the long winter of the Continental army at Valley Forge.

Lectures Eighteen and Nineteen describe the French alliance and the decision of France to intervene in the American war, the expansion of the war around the globe as an infant American navy is developed, and the fateful decision of the British government to shift the bulk of its military resources to fighting the French for control of the West Indies. North America became, in effect, a sideshow to what quickly became a second Great War for empire. But it was a sideshow only from the imperial perspective. In Lectures Twenty and Twenty-One, we will see that the British, even though much reduced in their capacity to make war in North America, could still cause serious trouble for the Americans, as Sir Henry Clinton turned his military attention to the American South. Lecture Twenty-Two pauses to look at those who gambled on British victory and lost—Loyalists and Indians—those who remained loyal to the American cause and suffered for it, and those who betrayed it (in this case, Benedict Arnold). In Lecture Twenty-Three, we return to the British "Southern Strategy," only to find that the British were too thinly stretched to grasp victory, and instead the principal British Southern army was forced into humiliating surrender at Yorktown. Lecture Twenty-Four takes a final look at the war as a world conflict, how the British Parliament finally declared that the war in America was unwinnable, how peace was negotiated, and what happened to the Revolutionary generation once its work was done.

The American Revolution was the greatest political irruption of modern times—"modern" meaning the centuries from the end of the Reformation and the beginning of the Enlightenment until now. It attempted, for the first time, to give political shape to the intellectual breakthroughs the Enlightenment had created in religion, science, economics, and literature. Its passionate devotion to demand *rights* rather than deference to *status* represented a decisive break with every notion of society that had prevailed since the Roman Empire. The people who fought against it—starting with the Loyalists and the British armies—were neither evil nor cunning; many of them, in fact, sympathized with the American cause. But they were hamstrung in their struggle "to keep the past upon its throne" by the sheer distance existing between Britain and the colonies at its periphery.

Both sides fought their way through the Revolution in remarkably similar, and conventional, ways. The decisive factor, in military terms, would turn out to be the French intervention, less for what it gave the Americans directly than for the distraction it gave the British. Along the way, we will meet a most remarkable cast of characters—perhaps the most remarkable ever assembled at one time in America—and especially George Washington, the indispensable man, who won a war, not with dash or genius, but with patience and cunning. And we will also meet the British cast—one of the most unhappy collections of talented but inadequate leaders who ever came together in one decade of British history: King George III, convinced that the slightest concession to the Americans would mean the disintegration of his empire; the Howe brothers, calm, brave, competent, and sure that military victory in North America was impossible for Britain; and Lord George Germain, who insisted on war in order to wipe out the stain of personal cowardice. And through it all we will include in our reckoning the players of the vast and varied roles of Indian chiefs (Joseph Brant), radical journalists (Thomas Paine), militiamen (those who ran as well as those who stood and fought), runaway slaves (Col. Tye), and German mercenaries (Johann Ewald).

It is the story of how the American nation was made—by ideas and by words, by combat and by endurance, by very ordinary and very extraordinary men and women. This is, as it turns out, also the way we have remade it in every American generation.

Note: Many quoted passages in this course reflect the spelling and punctuation of the colonial era.

Lecture One
The Imperial Crisis, 1763–1773

Scope: For decades after the first colonies were established, the king and the Church of England were largely content to neglect them. All along, Americans thought of themselves as fully English; after all, they had fought side by side with the British in the French and Indian War. That very war, however, had brought Britain close to financial collapse, so in 1765 Parliament passed the Stamp Act to force Americans to shoulder their share of the burden of victory. The North American colonists were outraged at such taxation without representation. The Stamp Act was repealed, but Parliament taxed a variety of other commodities. Finally, Parliament repealed all offensive taxes except on tea—a move that led to the Boston Tea Party of 1773.

Outline

I. In this series of 24 lectures, we will discuss not so much the economics or ideology or politics of the American Revolution as the Revolution's mechanics as an armed uprising against the most dominant military power in the world.

    A. The first two lectures will cover the causes that impelled us to a separation with the British Empire, and in Lecture Three, we study the British army of the 18th century.

    B. Lectures Four through Eight review the first part of the Revolution, followed in Lecture Nine with a brief turn to the movement toward independence.

    C. Lectures Ten through Twelve address the campaigns of 1776, while Lecture Thirteen deals with the unhappy civilian-military relationship between Congress and the Continental army.

    D. Lectures Fourteen through Seventeen reveal the disasters and triumphs that befell the American cause, ending with the Valley Forge winter of 1777 to 1778.

    E. In Lectures Eighteen through Twenty-One, the scope of the war widens to include France. We also see that the war in North America loses none of its desperation, especially for the losers whom we'll meet in Lecture Twenty-Two: Indians, Loyalists, mutinous soldiers, a traitorous general, and a British spy.

F. In the final two lectures, we look at the critical American victory at Yorktown, and the way the peace was constructed and what became of people who had made both the war and the peace.

II. We start in 1763 in what was the high summer of what we may now call the "first British Empire."

    A. The first colonies were established as private commercial ventures, some covers used by religious and political dissidents.

    B. The colonies were left to run themselves.
        1. They invented their own local legislatures.
        2. They set up their own churches.
        3. They formed their own armed militias.

    C. So long as the colonies presented no expense to the royal treasury, the king and the Church of England were largely content to neglect them.

    D. This attitude of "salutary neglect" persisted until 1660, when the home government realized that the colonies now posed a threat to the balance of the British economy.
        1. Between 1663 and 1772, American purchases of British goods rose from 3 percent of all British exports to nearly 50 percent, and one-third of all British imports came from America.
        2. Almost one-third of Britain's merchant fleet had been constructed in its American colonies.
        3. Immigration from Britain and the German states and a healthy birthrate had increased the work force from 250,000 in 1700 to almost 2 million by 1763.

    E. Beginning in 1660, the home government began imposing new regulations on colonial trade, including the first comprehensive Navigation Act (1660), the Wool Act (1699), the Molasses Act (1733), and the Iron Acts (1750 and 1757).

    F. At first, few Americans balked.
        1. The costs could be passed off to consumers.
        2. Smuggling could get around the import regulations.
       3. They took the regulations as indicating that the colonies had come of age.

G. Americans thought of themselves as fully and properly English.
    1. Americans fought side by side with the British in the Seven Years' War, known in America as the French and Indian War.
    2. Americans rejoiced to have played a role in the British victory.

III. The Seven Years' War had left Britain victorious but near financial collapse.

    A. Imperial planners saw the Americans prospering under English government and concluded that it was time to levy direct taxes on the colonies' interior economies, as had long been done in England.

    B. In 1765, Parliament passed a Stamp Act for the colonies, requiring all legal documents, newspapers, college diplomas, and other products of the print trade to display a revenue stamp.

IV. At that point, the lid blew off everything in America.

    A. The North American colonies had developed ad hoc legislatures of their own. These legislatures were the only places where the colonists felt their interests were represented, as none of the colonies was entitled to send representatives to sit in Parliament in London.

    B. The Stamp Act did not last long.
        1. Mobs threatened Stamp Act agents.
        2. Clubs and societies calling themselves the Loyal Nine or the Sons of Liberty staged mock burials of the corpse of Liberty.
        3. The colonies convened a Stamp Act Congress to determine a joint response in October 1765.
        4. Colonial merchants were dragooned into agreeing to boycott British imports.

    C. By March 1766, members of Parliament finally arranged for repeal, but in their retreat, they passed the Declaratory Act, insisting on the principle of Parliament's right to pass legislation—including tax legislation—for the colonies.
        1. The language of the Declaratory Act suggested that the colonies were no more than settlements.
        2. It suggested that the colonists lacked all the rights to self-government that the English had at home.

V. In 1767, Parliament tried again to impose a scheme of taxes on the colonial economies, in the form of duties on a variety of imported commodities. This attempt further inflamed the situation.

    A. A new system of customs officers provoked confrontations in colonial ports.

    B. On March 5, 1770, the 29th Regiment opened fire on a Boston crowd that had attacked them with stones, ice balls, and chunks of firewood; five Americans were killed.

    C. Parliament repealed the offensive taxes except on tea.

        1. The tax on tea was a way to assist another colonial venture, the East India Company and to assert Parliament's right to govern the colonies.

        2. On the night of December 16, 1773, a group of Boston's Sons of Liberty, disguised as Mohawk Indians, boarded three merchant ships and pitched the contents of 342 chests of East India Company tea into Boston Harbor.

Suggested Reading:

Greene, *Pursuits of Happiness*, chap. 8.

Nash, *The Urban Crucible*, chap. 11.

Weintraub, *Iron Tears*, chap. 1.

Questions to Consider:

1. What forced Great Britain to change its attitude toward its colonies?

2. What was the legal status of the colonial assemblies?

Lecture Two
The Ancient Constitution

Scope: Through the centuries, the British monarchy had begun to lose power to the Parliament, where, in the time of the Hanoverians, the House of Commons was divided into the Tories, who were loyal to the king, and the Whigs. Although the Hanoverian kings disliked the Whigs, it was the Whigs who had invited them to the throne, so they had to endure a succession of Whig-led governments. When the Seven Years' War ended, Hanoverian king George III, determined to impose his will on the Parliament and appointed a series of prime ministers to help him do so, ending finally in 1770 with Sir Frederick North, better known as Lord North.

Across the ocean, Americans saw Whig John Locke's account of the creation of governments as a description of how their own societies and governments had come into being—America was for them the state of nature. King George III, Lord North, and the majority in Parliament saw things differently and chose to adopt a series of punitive measures in retaliation for the Boston Tea Party's wanton destruction of property. "Honest Tom" Gage was appointed military governor for Massachusetts, and believed he could bring order to the state. He was mistaken.

Outline

I. English society was composed of three orders: the monarchy, the nobility, and the common people, represented respectively by the king and, in Parliament, the House of Lords, and the House of Commons.

    A. During the Tudor dynasty of the 1500s, the monarch was the major player.

        1. Even though the king was supposed to be dependent on Parliament for money, both Henry VII and Henry VIII were rich enough on their own and did not have very much in the way of government that needed paying for.

        2. Consequently, Parliament had little actual power to restrain the king.

B. The nobility posed more of a threat to the king, so Henry VIII and Elizabeth I created a bureaucracy of professional civil servants who are entirely loyal and entirely dependent on the monarch's good will.

C. The easing out of the nobles from their role in government left a vacuum. James I, the first of the Stuart kings, ascended the throne after the death of Elizabeth, who had no children.

    1. James I planned to reshape English politics around the newly popular idea of kingly Absolutism.

    2. The chaos and instability that Europe suffered through the 1500s and 1600s, made this idea quite appealing.

D. When James's son Charles came to the throne in 1625, he found the gentry in the Commons difficult to deal with.

    1. They hemmed him in with statute law and refusals to vote for taxes.

    2. By 1642 he had provoked the Commons so greatly that they resorted to the sword, and the terrible English Civil Wars ensued.

    3. Charles I was seized, tried, and executed, and England became a republic, albeit briefly.

E. The Commons proved no better at ruling than the king had been.

    1. In the 1650s the country descended into military rule under the Puritan Oliver Cromwell.

    2. When Cromwell died in 1658, England invited the king's exiled son to return to England as Charles II.

    3. Charles II had learned his father's lesson to deal carefully with Parliament.

II. Charles's brother James inherited the throne in 1685, without having learned their father's lesson.

A. James imagined he could go back to the drawing board of Absolutism.

B. Parliament proceeded to teach the lesson all over again with the Glorious Revolution of 1688.

    1. With less bloodshed than the Civil Wars of 40 years before, they exiled James across the channel.

    2. In his place, Parliament invited James's daughter Mary and her Dutch husband, William of Orange, to rule, followed by Mary's sister Anne.

    3. When Anne died childless in 1714, Parliament invited another foreign prince, George, the Elector of Hanover and Duke of Brunswick-Luneburg, to reign as George I.

III. It was now clear who had the upper hand, and it was neither the king nor the nobility.

    A. Theoretically, the king was ruler of all he surveyed.
        1. He was chief of the British army and navy.
        2. He was head of the Church.
        3. He was sovereign of a united kingdom of England, Scotland, Wales, and Ireland.

    B. In practice, his powers were limited.
        1. He had only a veto power over Parliamentary legislation, which he dared not use.
        2. He could choose his great officers of state from whatever party or faction in Parliament held the upper political hand against the others.

IV. The two most general divisions in the House of Commons were the Whigs and the Tories.

    A. The Tories were loyal to the king and the Church and to holding onto the remains of the nobility's economic power, and they believed that Britain was going to the dogs.

    B. The Whigs were distinguished by factionalism and ideological complexity.
        1. They saw themselves as the upright party of country living.
        2. They were the party of those who loved the Protestant religion.
        3. The Whigs also possessed the most talented political thinkers, such as John Locke, James Harrington, John Trenchard, Thomas Gordon, and Joseph Addison.
        4. They saw themselves as the party of virtue and the Tories as the party of power.

V. The Hanoverian kings, George I, George II, and George III, naturally disliked the pretensions of the Whigs.

    A. However, it was the Whigs who had invited German George I to the throne in the first place, so the Hanoverians had to endure a succession of Whig-led governments.

B. The Whigs took full advantage of this by casting themselves as the saviors of England whenever things had run into a muddle.

VI. By the 1770s, the "great offices of state" had grown into a mazy bureaucracy.

    A. The principal office was that of first lord of the treasury, nominally the king's "prime minister."

    B. The treasury was then followed by the three secretaries of state: for the Northern Department (diplomatic correspondence with northern Europe), the Southern Department, and the American colonies.

    C. Military forces were divided between the first lord of the admiralty and the commander in chief of the army.

    D. These were followed by seven other offices of lesser stature.

    E. The real power lay with the prime minister, the secretaries of state, and the heads of the army and navy.

VII. When the Seven Years' War ended, George III had been on the throne for three years and could see where the drift of events was taking Parliamentary politics, and he determined above all things to impose his will on the drift.

    A. He forced William Pitt's resignation as secretary of state for the Southern department and replaced him with his beloved mentor, John Stuart, the 3rd Earl of Bute.

        1. Bute's ministry was brief and disastrous. He was succeeded by George Grenville.

        2. Grenville devised the Stamp Act, and its impending failure pulled him down in 1765.

    B. The king then turned to Pitt and to Charles Watson-Wentworth, the 2nd Marquess of Rockingham, for a new government.

        1. Pitt was sick and struggling, so *de facto* power fell into the hands of Charles Townsend, Chancellor of the Exchequer.

        2. Townsend self-destructed by designing the elaborate tax plan for the colonies that resulted in the Boston Massacre in 1770.

    C. In 1770, the king got a prime minister he could really appreciate in Sir Frederick North, better known as Lord North.

VIII. The Americans did not see matters as the Whigs did.

    A. While the Whigs liked to see themselves as the "country party" they had been the government for most of the preceding half-century, and their leaders were only occasionally drawn from the commoners.

    B. While John Locke had based Whig political theory on compacts made by people emerging from a "state of nature," no one in England had ever seen a state of nature.

    C. The Americans looked at Locke and the Whigs through the other end of the telescope.

        1. In America, nine-tenths of the colonists were farmers and really were "the country."

        2. Three-quarters of the colonists were descendants of radical religious dissenters who had long ago concluded that England was a moral quagmire.

        3. Americans recoiled in distaste at the low-life characters England shipped to the colonies as soldiers and officials.

    D. When Locke talked about governments emerging from a "state of nature" he imagined he was inviting his readers to a thought experiment.

        1. In a state of nature, people banded together and created a government. It was the people who created the government from the ground up, not from the top down.

        2. Americans read this account of the creation of government, as a description of how their own societies and governments had come into being; America was for them the state of nature, and the colonial governments that they had created while the Crown was practicing "salutary neglect" were their own to change as they pleased.

        3. For an Englishman, Locke was a mere hypothesis; for Americans, Locke was drawing from real life.

IX. King George III, Lord North, and the majority in Parliament did not view matters in this way.

    A. They were horrified at the Boston Tea Party's wanton destruction of property.

    B. The secretary of state for the colonies, William Legge, 2nd Earl of Dartmouth, advised Lord North to punish Boston by removing its custom house and holding its assembly elsewhere.

C. Parliament adopted three punitive measures known as the Intolerable Acts, designed to hold up Boston as an example to the rest of British America.
   1. The Boston Port Bill closed the port of Boston to all traffic until restitution was made for the destruction of the tea.
   2. The Impartial Administration of Justice Act provided for the trials of colonials—especially those indicted for the Boston riot—outside of Massachusetts.
   3. The Bill for Better Regulating the Government of Massachusetts Bay annulled the colony's charter and put it under direct Crown control.
D. A military governor was appointed for Massachusetts, the commander in chief for North America, Maj. Gen. Thomas Gage.
   1. Gage was the younger son of a family that had been staunch royalists since the Civil Wars.
   2. During the French and Indian War, he survived a major ambush at the Battle of the Monongahela River in 1755 while under the command of Edward Braddock, and he won a series of promotions, rising to the rank of major general.
   3. In 1758 he married an American wife, Margaret Kemble.
   4. At the war's end he was appointed commander in chief of the postwar forces in America in 1763.

Suggested Reading:

Bailyn, *Ideological Origins of the American Revolution*.

Gipson, *The Triumphant Empire: Thunder-Clouds Gather in the West*, chap. 13.

Jensen, *The Founding of a Nation*, chap. 17.

Questions to Consider:

1. How would you characterize the succession of British prime ministers between 1760 and 1770?

2. Why did the Whig theory of government resonate so strongly with Americans?

Lecture Three
"A Soldier What's Fit for a Soldier"

Scope: The average British soldier was young, likely out of work, and illiterate. He was paid little, trained minimally, disciplined severely, and retained for life. On the other hand, officers, who bought their commissions, were drawn entirely from the class of gentlemen. Both officers and men wore a red wool coat whose purpose was both identification (each regiment had different colors on lapels and cuffs) and intimidation in battle. The system of the regiment, the primary building block of the British army, dated back to the 1640s and 1650s. The British soldier's principal weapon was the Short Land Service musket or "Brown Bess," a flintlock, single-shot, muzzle-loading, .75-calibre musket. Although it was not particularly accurate, when used in mass volleys, it confused and demoralized the enemy and made way for the real lethal weapon of the time, the bayonet.

Outline

I. "Honest Tom" Gage was in England when news of the Boston Tea Party arrived and was summoned by King George III for consultation.

   A. Gage believed that dealing with the Americans would not be expensive and that four regiments sent to Boston would do the trick.

   B. Gage was to implement the closure of the port of Boston and the reorganization of the Massachusetts colonial government.

   C. If all went well, all of the colonial governments could be remodeled on the same pattern.

   D. The king equipped Gage with the 4th, 5th, 38th, and 43rd regiments and directed them all to Boston.

II. Who were the British soldiers that arrived in Boston in June 1774?

   A. The customary image of the British soldier of the Revolution is that of a collection of Britain's dregs, but the reality is somewhat different.

   1. The average British soldier was probably about 23 years old and about 5-foot-6-inches in height.

2. He had most probably been an agricultural laborer; weavers and shoemakers made up the next largest categories.
3. It was a volunteer army; the average soldier probably enlisted because he was out of work.
4. He was as likely to be Scottish or Irish as he was to be English.
5. He was probably illiterate.

B. The enlistment bounty was a guinea and a crown.
1. The soldier's pay was eight pence a day, subject to "stoppages" for uniforms, tools, and such, thus reducing it to almost nothing.
2. Soldiers could earn extra pay for various tasks and in peacetime could work civilian jobs in their off-hours.

C. Strictly speaking, no one enlisted in the British army; they enlisted or were recruited for service in a particular regiment, the basic organizational unit of the army.
1. Unless a regiment was on foreign service, the recruit usually joined it at once and underwent basic training.
2. Training was not very arduous; the bulk of the recruit's education was in drill.
3. Enlistment was for life.

D. Discipline was severe but was held to be necessary for proper behavior and subordination.
1. Flogging was not abolished until 1881.
2. Desertion, cowardice, striking an officer, mutiny, murder, and rape were all flogging or hanging offenses.
3. Lesser offenses could be punished by solitary confinement, riding a wooden horse, caning or beating, or name-calling.

E. Officers were drawn entirely from the class of gentlemen.
1. Like the ranks, they were almost equally divided among Scots, Irish, and English.
2. There was no military academy for officers until the establishment of Sandhurst in 1796; most officers bought their commissions at prices that kept the lower classes out.
3. The lowest officer rank, ensign, cost £400, and every grade upward had to be bought with subsequent purchases.

F. Officers and men stood out together because of their uniform, a "full-bodied" red wool coat.

    1. The coat featured a divided rear skirt, oversize folded-back cuffs, and folded-back lapels and skirt-corners.

    2. The uniform included a sleeveless white vest, reaching down to the waist or the upper thigh, white knee-breeches, knee-high gaiters, and a wool-felt brimmed black hat.

G. The purposes of the uniform were identification and intimidation.

    1. Identification meant each regiment was entitled to adopt a distinctive color for the lapel and cuff facings of its uniforms.

    2. Intimidation is what came into play on the battlefield, advancing in lurid red.

III. The regiment was the primary building block of the British army.

    A. No formal organization existed above its level, though regiments could be grouped together as a brigade on an ad hoc basis for war service or for particular campaigns.

    B. There was only one grade of officer above the regimental command rank of colonel, and that was simply general.

    C. The regimental system was not that old, dating back to the English Civil Wars of the 1640s and 1650s.

        1. Oliver Cromwell's New Model Army of 1644 created a standing system of regiments.

        2. After the restoration of the monarchy in 1660, a number of these regiments were taken over into permanent service.

    D. Each regiment was to be divided into eight battalion companies, along with a grenadier company and a light infantry company.

        1. The battalion companies, each with three officers, three sergeants, three corporals, and 56 privates, were the principal fighting components of the regiment.

        2. Grenadiers were originally grenade-men—experts with hand grenades—but by the 1750s had developed into elite assault troops.

        3. The light companies carried lesser and lighter equipment and were usually assigned the job of skirmishers or as flankers.

        4. By 1774, the jobs of the grenadier and light infantry had blended together, as fast-moving shock troops.

E. The total number of regiments, and of the soldiers in them, fluctuated wildly. At the beginning of the Seven Years' War, the total strength of the army was only about 24,000 men.

    1. Parliament begrudged every penny spent on the army.

    2. The outbreak of the Seven Years' War prompted a massive military build-up to the unprecedented level of 203,000 men; 32 regiments containing 30,000 men were posted to the American theater of war.

    3. As soon as the war ended, the cutbacks began, and only a token presence remained in major American outposts.

IV. The British soldier's principal weapon was the Short Land Service musket, or "Brown Bess," first introduced in 1718.

    A. It was a musket that featured a 3-foot-6-inch-long barrel with no rifling and was utterly unreliable for hitting targets at more than 80 yards.

    B. It was bored for .75 calibre ammunition that crushed bone and tissue.

    C. It was a single-shot, muzzle-loader that had to be manually loaded and reloaded each time it was discharged.

    D. It was a flintlock; the mechanism for firing was a single integrated system consisting of a trigger, a hammer, a flint, and a frizzen.

    E. Flintlock muskets' technological limitations dictated that the fire not be wasted in individual target shooting but used in massed volleys that opened the way for the real decider of battle in the 1700s, the 17-inch-long bayonet.

Suggested Reading:

Reid, *British Redcoat, 1740–1793.*

Shy, *Toward Lexington*, chap. 7.

Stephenson, *Patriot Battles*, chap. 3.

Questions to Consider:

1. How does the real image of the 18th-century "redcoat" clash with the mythological image?

2. How was the British regiment deployed for battle?

Lecture Four
"How the British Regulars Fired and Fled"

Scope: Soon after returning to Boston, Thomas Gage saw that dealing with the Americans would be far more difficult than he had anticipated, and he asked the king for 20,000 men to control the situation, of which he was sent but a fraction. After the meeting of the First Continental Congress, however, the king promised Gage ample reinforcements and three new generals. Gage's initial inaction irritated his men, but the action soon began in April 1776, when the first clashes between the British and rebel militia took place at Lexington and Concord, where the British sorely underestimated the abilities of the American militia. The British took a terrible beating. News of the fight at Lexington and Concord resulted in a flood of militia volunteers coming to Boston just when Gage's new British generals arrived, bent on sorting out the situation.

Outline

I. With the return of Thomas Gage and the arrival of new British regiments, Boston had the largest concentration of British military force on the continent.

    A. After the Massachusetts legislature reelected Samuel Adams as clerk of the House of Representatives, Gage carried out his orders.

        1. Henceforth, the legislature would meet in Salem, not Boston.

        2. Gage would veto the appointment of any officers suspected of having a hand in the Tea Party.

    B. The Massachusetts House promptly responded with a boycott of British goods.

        1. Gage retaliated by canceling the proposed meeting of the legislature in Salem.

        2. The legislature called its own session to meet in Cambridge and resumed all the functions of the old legislature, including a secret authorization for buying arms and ammunition.

    C. Gage sent a battalion to seize the provincial gunpowder stores in the Provincial Powder House, only to find that militia units had been withdrawing powder all summer.

D. More alarming was the reaction of the colony.
  1. Signal fires were lit and militia units were called out.
  2. Cambridge Loyalists fled to Boston.
  3. In Boston, a committee was formed under Paul Revere to monitor future British troop movements in and out of Boston.
  4. In Rhode Island, the militia seized the artillery in Fort George.
  5. In Portsmouth, New Hampshire, 400 militiamen stormed Fort William and Mary and took 100 barrels of gunpowder.
  6. In February 1775, when Gage again attempted to seize colonial weapons and stores at Salem, a battalion of the 64th Regiment of Foot was forced to withdraw by militia.

E. Gage began to have second thoughts about dealing with the Americans.
  1. He began constructing defenses across Boston Neck on September 2.
  2. He got only a fraction of the 20,000 men he had requested from the king and the Earl of Dartmouth.

II. Colonial legislatures up and down the Atlantic seaboard passed resolutions in support of the Bostonians.

  A. Where royal governors tried to suppress the resolutions, the legislatures reconvened themselves as provincial congresses.

  B. The members of the Virginia House of Burgesses called for a "general congress" of all the colonies in Philadelphia, resulting in the meeting of the First Continental Congress on September 5, 1774.
  1. It swore continued loyalty to the Crown but also recognized the Massachusetts Provincial Congress as the legitimate government of Massachusetts.
  2. It called for more boycotts and invited the Quebec province to join them.
  3. It drew up a bill of grievances to submit to the king.

  C. The king reacted by sending General Gage reinforcements.
  1. He was sent nine regiments and battalions from two others, plus his contingent of marines.
  2. He also got three new generals: William Howe, John Burgoyne, and Henry Clinton.

III. Gage's inaction soon angered even the officers, but he was secretly scouting the area and began to plan to seize the colonial munitions at Concord.

    A. On April 14, 1775, Gage received orders from the Earl of Dartmouth to arrest the participants in the Provincial Congress, which he attempted to carry out.

    B. By the time he carried it out, almost every detail of his search-and-destroy mission was already known by the Americans.

        1. On April 15, the Provincial Congress in Worcester adjourned.

        2. Select companies of the town militias were to remain on 24-hour alert as "minutemen."

        3. In Concord, people began moving the military supplies out of the town, and Paul Revere, William Dawes, and Samuel Prescott rode over the roads that led to Lexington and Concord.

        4. Revere and Dawes reached Lexington sometime after midnight on April 19 and roused Adams and Hancock as well as the Lexington militia.

        5. Halfway to Concord, Revere was caught by Gage's advance screen, and Dawes, narrowly escaping capture, turned back to Lexington. Prescott raised the alarm in Concord just before 2 am.

    C. The British marched through Cambridge, turning northwest toward Lexington.

        1. It was clear that all surprise had been lost; the British advance guard led by Maj. Pitcairn could hear bells and warning shots and see signal beacons in the distance.

        2. Beside the town's common, Pitcairn's light infantry faced 60 to 70 Lexington militiamen.

        3. The meeting was unexpected, and officers on both sides urged calm and also resolution.

        4. However, someone fired either without orders or accidentally, resulting in the light infantry killing several Lexington men and wounding many others.

    D. Col. Smith, arriving at Lexington Common, called his companies back to order and put his men on the road back to Concord.

    E. Once in town, Smith sent seven companies of light infantry across the North Bridge to establish a protective west-facing line.

F. In their haste, the British paid no attention to the gathering of a sizeable number of militiamen to the north, on Punkatasset Hill, where five companies had hurriedly assembled, commanded by Col. Barrett.

G. The British did not think the militia posed much of a threat—probably the single greatest mistake the British would make in the conflict.

H. James Barrett marched his men through a ridge 300 yards west of the North Bridge, shook them out into line of battle, and had them load their muskets.

    1. Barrett put his companies into column and began marching down by divisions, to the North Bridge.

    2. The British light infantry at the bridge fired a volley, killing the captain of the Acton militia.

    3. The militia waited until they had closed to 50 yards, then fired a volley that knocked down half of the eight British officers, killed three rankers, and wounded nine more.

    4. Under the weight of the militia fire, the British gave way and fled.

I. Back in Concord, Col. Smith heard volley firing and took two of his grenadier companies out to the bridge. Around noon on April 19, he turned the head of his column back toward Boston. He almost didn't make it.

    1. Fresh militia companies continued to show up, and they took up positions at choke points along the road to harass the British.

    2. When the column reached the outskirts of Lexington, the Lexington militia were ready with another ambush.

J. By around 2 pm, just when the exhausted, disorganized British were running low on ammunition, they came upon the 4th, 23rd, and 47th regiments and the Royal Marines under the command of Lord Percy.

    1. Percy extricated the survivors of the expedition.

    2. Seventy-three British officers and rankers had been killed, 174 wounded, and 25 missing.

    3. The American militia lost 50 dead and 39 wounded.

IV. Word of the fight at Lexington and Concord flew rapidly out to the other colonies throughout New England and southward.

    A. A flood of militia volunteers from all over New England flowed toward Boston.

    B. Gage could scarcely believe he was under siege and failed to declare martial law.

    C. On May 25, Gage's new subordinates—Howe, Burgoyne, and Clinton—arrived, ready to take charge.

Suggested Reading:

Fischer, *Paul Revere's Ride*, chaps. 13–15.

Gross, *The Minutemen and Their World*, chap. 5.

Shy, "Thomas Gage," in Billias, *George Washington's Generals and Opponents.*

Questions to Consider:

1. What misconceptions have sprung up about how the Americans fought at Lexington and Concord?

2. How did the rebels in the colonies circumvent the efforts of royal governors to shut down the colonial legislatures?

Lecture Five
Standoff in Boston, 1775

Scope: Although the new Continental army was challenging to recruit and organize, Thomas Gage found it far more difficult to recruit and replace the British troops he had lost. In addition, many members of Parliament opposed the war that King George so adamantly supported. Meanwhile, the conflict began to spread with the American capture of a British post at Ticonderoga.

On the same day, John Adams's proposal to the Second Continental Congress to declare the colonies "free, sovereign and independent states" was met with horror by many of his fellow delegates, for whom reconciliation was the overwhelming desire. The Second Continental Congress also authorized the creation of a combined colonial army, with George Washington as commander in chief and senior general. Washington knew the hardship of war as well as the hardship of being a gentleman farmer who, like many, had to deal not only with threat of what the king's men might do but also with what their own slaves might do if incited to rebel.

Outline

I. When the Provincial Congress reassembled on April 21, it had to create a Continental army, and what they came up with was a mirror image of the British system.

   A. But the militiamen were used to their local companies and officers, and reshuffling them into regiments and creating accurate rolls took longer than expected.

      1. The Provincial Congress had authority only over the Massachusetts militia and could to nothing about the militia units that had joined from Rhode Island, Connecticut, and New Hampshire.

      2. Fitting the militia companies into regiments was like trying to piece together parts from different puzzles.

      3. The camps were disorderly, and the regiments so unevenly filled that recruiting parties had to be sent out into the countryside.

B. On April 20, the president of the Provincial Congress's Committee of Safety sent a letter to Gage suggesting everyone talk matters over.

C. Gage was having difficulties making up his mind.

    1. On one hand, he immediately moved to disarm the civilian population of the city.

    2. On the other hand, he waited until June 12 to declare martial law.

D. Gage was convinced that he had too few soldiers to attempt further operations outside Boston.

    1. From Lexington and Concord he realized that every rebel could be replaced locally, but every redcoat lost was replaceable only by a three-month-long transatlantic process.

    2. New orders authorized him four more infantry regiments, so he felt there was no point in taking further action until those troops arrived.

II. Gage was not the only Englishman who was surprised and uncertain.

A. When Parliament met in mid-January, 1775, it was clear that many members were uneasy about the Intolerable Acts.

    1. On February 1, William Pitt asked for suspension of the acts and recognition of the say of colonial legislatures in all tax matters.

    2. Sir Charles Pratt supported Pitt's plea and called the Intolerable Acts a "Bill of war."

B. Some senior serving officers gave notice that they would not serve in an American war.

C. Merchants hurt by boycotts of their products begged for restoration of commerce.

D. Even within Lord North's cabinet, the Earl of Dartmouth thought Chatham's plan was worth considering.

E. The king, however, was adamant, and Parliament would swing behind him and Lord North.

    1. An address to the king, assuring him full support in Parliament, passed the House of Commons.

    2. In November, the Earl of Dartmouth was replaced as secretary of state for America by a militant hardliner, Lord George Germain.

III. Meanwhile, the conflict began to spread beyond New England.

    A. The Congress's Committee of Safety authorized Benedict Arnold to recruit a regiment of volunteers and raid the tumble-down British post at Ticonderoga in western Massachusetts and seize the weaponry there.

    B. When he arrived, he learned that the Green Mountain Boys, commanded by Ethan Allen, had a similar mission.

        1. Arnold overtook Allen 20 miles from Ticonderoga and struck a deal. Allen would allow Arnold to share command of an attack.

        2. At daybreak on May 10, 1775, 83 Green Mountain Boys surprised the corporal's guard at Ticonderoga and seized the supplies.

IV. On the same day, at a Second Continental Congress, Massachusetts delegate John Adams proposed that the Congress ought to declare the colonies "free, sovereign and independent states."

    A. This opinion was received with horror by his fellow delegates, for reconciliation on equitable terms, not independence, was the overwhelming desire of the Continental Congress.

    B. On May 16, Richard Henry Lee moved that Congress authorize the creation of a combined colonial army, "the American Continental army," specifying four major generals and making George Washington, commander in chief and senior general.

V. Born in 1732, Washington had never really wanted to be anything but a soldier.

    A. When his half-brother, Lawrence, a regimental captain, died in 1752, George inherited the estate and his brother's post.

        1. Within two years he was appointed lieutenant colonel and sent by the royal governor of Virginia to clear the French out of some land that Virginia claimed near the forks of the Ohio River.

        2. This incident triggered the French and Indian War, and opened up a great opportunity for Washington when General Edward Braddock invited him to join staff of two regiments of British infantry, sent over to deal with the French.

        3. Braddock and his troops met with disaster at the hands of the French and the Indians in an ambush at the battle of Monongahela. Washington took command of the Virginia militia accompanying Braddock and covered the retreat of the regulars.

    4. The action made Washington into a hero, but no further action or permanent confirmation of his temporary rank of captain were forthcoming.

  B. In 1759, he married a wealthy widow, Martha Dandridge Custis, took his seat in the Virginia House of Burgesses, and retired to the life of a gentleman farmer.

VI. Washington soon learned the hardships of being a Virginia planter.

  A. The imperial government had restricted the purchase and development of new land in the west.

  B. The new taxes of the 1760s, beginning with the Stamp Act, alienated Washington still more.

  C. In 1774, he was selected as one of the Virginia delegates to the First Continental Congress.

VII. A well-to-do Virginia planter had a great deal at stake in defying the authority of the British Crown, but the planters' apprehension of what the king's men might do was not as great as their fear of what their own slaves might do.

  A. Slave labor had been part of colonial life for 150 years, the ugly secret at the foundation of American prosperity.

  B. Slavery was fed by a highly lucrative flow of captive Africans across the Atlantic.

  C. The British North American colonies received only about 10 percent of the 11 million Africans transported to the New World between 1500 and 1830, but black slavery was present in each colony.

VIII. Slaves accounted for 20 percent of the population of the 13 colonies.

  A. They were an asset and a threat—indispensable labor with the threat of revolt.

  B. To rebel would be to risk losing the support every planter would enjoy from the British regulars in the event of a slave uprising—unless the British were inciting the uprising themselves.

  C. Two days after Lexington and Concord, the royal governor of Virginia, John Murray, 4th Earl of Dunmore, attempted to raid the colonial powder magazine at Williamsburg.

D. When militia mustered across the colony and threatened to march to Williamsburg, Dunmore himself threatened to arm his own slaves and any others who joined him.

   E. In November, Dunmore issued a proclamation declaring he would free any slave who agreed to bear arms on the Royalist side.

   F. This proclamation brought many of Virginia's undecided gentry over to the Continental Congress's side.

IX. Washington arrived in Philadelphia in May for the opening of the Second Continental Congress, wearing his old uniform.

   A. Washington had the requisite military experience and represented the interests of the largest of the colonies.

   B. Congress offered him command of the Continental army—which did not yet exist.

   C. He set out for Boston, where the new army was embroiled with the British at Bunker Hill.

Suggested Reading:

Nash, *The Unknown American Revolution*, chap. 4.

Rakove, *The Beginnings of National Politics*, chaps. 3–4.

Randall, *George Washington*, chaps. 10–12.

Questions to Consider:

1. What role did American slavery play in driving the Virginians into the arms of the rebellion?

2. How important was the attitude of the king in forming the British response?

Lecture Six
Bunker Hill

Scope: After Thomas Gage's long awaited British reinforcements finally
arrived in Boston, he was ready to strike. The Americans, however,
got wind of his plans and quickly produced a remarkably
professional fortification on Breed's Hill. With British men ready
to move forward, the question in the air was whether the rebel
militiamen could stand up to the British regulars. The answer came
after the order to fire when close to 100 of British general Howe's
men were killed outright. The next time the British surged forward,
however, the American militia turned and fled. When Washington
later arrived in Boston, instead of finding an army suffering from
the sting of defeat, he found disorganization, no supplies,
quarrelling officers, and an unjustified confidence in the militias'
abilities. More troubling he found a general reluctance of these
American soldiers to put aside their regional alliances and become
part of a national army.

Outline

I. The geography of Boston made it a splendid port but a terrible fort.

   A. Boston sat atop a peninsula in its broad, open harbor.
      1. But this tiny-necked peninsula had only a meager moat. Along
         its southeast side, the Dorchester heights were less than a mile
         away, placing the town in range of bombardment.
      2. On the tip of another small peninsula facing Boston was
         Charlestown, behind which rose a succession of three hills:
         Morton's Hill, Breed's Hill, and Bunker Hill, where the
         Charlestown peninsula was attached to the mainland. Even
         moderate artillery could drop solid shot into the town and into
         the midst of British admiral Samuel Graves' flotilla in Boston
         Harbor.

   B. Graves saw the danger posed by the Charlestown hills and asked
      Thomas Gage to post a regiment there. Gage chose to await
      reinforcements.

   C. On May 27, a party of Massachusetts and New Hampshire forces
      seized Noddle Island, across to the northeast from Boston.

1. Gage sent a small contingent of British marines aboard the converted schooner *Diana* to clear the Americans off.
2. During the firefight between the Marines and the militia, the Americans forced the *Diana* to run aground, boarded her, and burned her in full view of the British garrison.
3. The next morning the American cannon put so many holes in the sloop *Britannia* that she had to be towed out of range.

D. To Gage's advantage, the Americans had no long-range siege guns.
   1. The American commanders were also reluctant to seem too aggressive and thereby sacrifice their claim to being innocent victims of British tyranny.
   2. By the end of May, Gage also had his reinforcements and William Howe, Henry Clinton, and John Burgoyne to lead them.

E. Gage was ready to strike on June 18, depositing the bulk of the troops under Henry Clinton at Lechmere Point, opposite the rebels' camp at Cambridge; another 1,500 under William Howe would seize the Dorchester heights and head up through Roxbury to smash the Americans.

F. Word of these plans had swiftly leaked out. After weeks of delay, the Massachusetts Provincial Congress's Committee of Safety and its president, Dr. Joseph Warren, resolved that Bunker Hill should be securely kept and defended.
   1. Three Massachusetts regiments, along with 200 of Israel Putnam's Connecticut militia and an artillery company, were sent to the Charlestown peninsula on the evening of June 16.
   2. After some uncertainty about what to do, they set to work to produce a remarkably professional fortification.
   3. By first light the oblong redoubt was nearing completion, armed with the 4-pounder guns taken off the *Diana* two weeks before.

G. That morning, Admiral Graves, seeing the redoubt, revised his attack plans.

H. By one o'clock, Howe had a strike force in navy longboats and landed his light infantry and grenadiers, plus the 5th, 38th, 43rd, and 52nd regiments on the Charlestown peninsula to attack the redoubt from behind.

I. Israel Putnam headed for Cambridge to collect reinforcements, most of whom managed to reach the peninsula just as Howe and senior officer Robert Pigot's men were ready to move forward.

J. The British officers, and probably the American officers, were unsure whether the rebel militiamen would stand up to the British regulars.

    1. The chief challenge for the American officers would be to restrain their own forces from firing as soon as they saw the British.

    2. Israel Putnam, arriving with reinforcements, told his men, "Don't fire till you see the whites of their eyes, then fire low," and advised them to pick off the commanders first.

    3. John Stark pounded stakes into the ground at 40 yards to mark the spot the British would have to cross before his men started firing.

    4. The British came, crossing Stark's stake line.

    5. The rebel order to fire came, and the rebel muskets roared.

    6. The British reeled and stopped. Of the 350 men in Howe's light infantry vanguard, 95 had been killed and dozens more were wounded and down.

    7. The British began to drop back by twos and threes; then they all turned and ran.

II. William Howe quickly formed up his elite flank companies and sent them back up to the stone wall.

    A. They reached the line marked by the dead of the first attack when the rebel muskets fired again.

        1. Hundreds of men went down, and the rest staggered back.

        2. Pigot pushed his regiments up the hill and they were mown down again.

        3. Howe called for Clinton's reserves to cross over to Charlestown, and Clinton rallied the fragments of Pigot's regiments.

    B. Howe did not know that the Americans were running out of ammunition, both for their artillery and their muskets.

        1. The volleys that had cut down Howe's light infantry had used up approximately 13,000 musket balls.

        2. Although the Americans' casualties were slight, the militiamen were exhausted, thirsty, and worried about their firepower.

C. The next time Howe and Clinton surged forward, Howe wheeled the 5th and 52nd regiments to the left so that the full weight of the British attack was concentrated on the redoubt.

    1. Now there were more British targets than the Americans could bring down.

    2. The Americans began scrambling over the rear walls of the redoubt and running toward Bunker Hill.

    3. They left 140 dead, with 271 wounded and 30 missing.

D. The British were, however, in no shape to pursue.

    1. Of the 2,300 soldiers funneled into the fight for Breed's Hill (or as it became known, Bunker Hill), 226 were dead and 828 wounded, more than 250 of whom would die of their wounds over the next few weeks.

    2. These losses were not easily replaceable across 3,000 miles of ocean, and they had hit the ranks of veteran officers that were trained professionals.

III. On the American side, instead of feeling like a humiliating defeat, Bunker Hill became a cause for self-congratulation.

A. This attitude would prove a stumbling block to George Washington, who rode into Cambridge on July 2 with a troop of cavalry and his commission to organize a regular Continental army.

    1. Washington assumed that the militiamen were as eager as he had been to become real soldiers.

    2. But such soldiers would not have buckled at the first charge.

    3. They would not have found themselves short of ammunition because a regularly organized ordnance staff would have supplied it.

    4. They would not have exhausted themselves digging a redoubt because there would be a specialty pioneer corps to do it for them.

    5. They would have been equipped with bayonets of their own.

B. What Washington found instead was disorganization, nonexistent supplies, quarrelling officers, and a wholly unjustified attitude that the ordinary militiaman was the apple of God's eye.

    1. The militia could not be relied on to stick around the camp or to be regular and disciplined when they were there.

    2. New England governors meddled in the officer appointments.

3. Washington had to persuade the militiamen to join the Continental regiments rather than disbanding and going home to brag.
C. He wanted to make it clear that the Continental army was a *national* army, not just a collection of state units.
   1. Washington intended that the Continental regiments would identify themselves by number, not by regional origins, but the militiamen did not show any eagerness to join up as Continental soldiers.
   2. Washington could prevail on only 9,600 of the 16,000 militia who had been in and around Cambridge through the summer of 1775.
   3. In every battle ahead of him, Washington would have to augment his meager supply of Continentals with callouts of state militia, and nearly every case, they would contrive to lose battles for him, mostly through organizational unpredictability.

Suggested Reading:

Fleming, *Now We Are Enemies*, chaps. 9–14.

Stephenson, *Patriot Battles*, chap. 13.

Wright, *The Continental Army*, chaps. 2–3.

Questions to Consider:

1. Does the result of Bunker Hill sustain or discount the reputation won by the militia at Lexington and Concord?
2. What factor made the British victory at Bunker Hill "dear-bought"?

Lecture Seven
The King, the Conqueror, and the Coward

Scope: In Philadelphia, the Second Continental Congress issued a Declaration of "Taking up Arms" as well as an Olive Branch Petition to the Crown, suggesting reconciliation, both of which the king refused outright. Instead the king and Parliament issued what were effectively declarations of war. The king then dismissed Thomas Gage and turned over command of the British military in Boston to William Howe. He also replaced the Earl of Dartmouth with Lord George Sackville Germain. Howe the Whig and Germain the hawk were an odd pair, but they agreed that America could best be conquered by striking a blow at either the rebel army or the rebel Congress and by urging the many Loyalist Americans to take over the work of pulling down the rebel government.

Outline

I. While the British were appalled by their victory at Bunker Hill, the Americans were exhilarated by their defeat. What they saw as a moral victory gave them a useful surge of self-confidence, but they took out of it some less useful lessons.

    A. They came away with the certainty that free-born militia were better, man for man, than an army of professional hirelings.

        1. They had not bolted at the first sign of the oncoming redcoats.

        2. They had inflicted great casualties, proving their superior marksmanship.

    B. In Philadelphia, the Second Continental Congress greeted the news of the Bunker Hill fight by issuing "A Declaration ... setting forth the Causes and Necessity of their taking up Arms" on July 6.

        1. The Declaration denied any intention of dissolving the union with Britain. But it declared the colonists were resolved to be free.

        2. The Declaration was followed on July 8 with a petition asking the king to suggest a means of reconciliation.

        3. This statement could be interpreted as an "olive branch," or as a firmly crafted statement of what the king's real alternatives were.

    C. What the militia and Congress had alike missed, in the first flush of pride, was that all the marksmanship and fortitude at Bunker Hill had gone for nothing.

        1. Their officers were prone to quarrelling with each other.

        2. They had no organized supply system to keep them fed with ammunition.

        3. Once things got into a pinch, they broke and ran.

II. In England, Bunker Hill produced exasperation rather than caution.

    A. Thomas Gage could report only minimal progress, a long list of killed and wounded, and recommend the employment of a large army, or, if not that, suspension of land operations and calling in the navy to blockade the America coast.

    B. Lord North advised the king to treat the standoff in America as a foreign war.

    C. The Earl of Dartmouth conceded that some additional land forces would be needed, to be followed in early spring with further commitments.

III. The arrival of the Continental Congress's Declaration on "Taking up Arms" and the Olive Branch Petition infuriated George III.

    A. On August 23 he issued his own proclamation declaring that the rebellion be suppressed and the traitors brought to justice.

        1. On October 26, Parliament seconded the proclamation with an "Act Prohibiting Trade and Intercourse with America," shutting down all trade and commerce with the 13 colonies represented by the Continental Congress and making all ships or vessels belonging to the colonies forfeited to the king.

        2. It was a declaration of war.

    B. The Americans were unmoved.

        1. The total effective force of the British army was only about 38,000 parceled out amongst stations around the world.

        2. The Royal Navy mustered only 18,000 sailors and 270 ships of various sizes and conditions.

        3. Like the army, the navy was spread around the world.

    C. Nevertheless, George III stood firm.

        1. He was prepared to strip the West India garrisons of their regiments and send them to Boston.

        2. And he set about recruiting mercenaries to fill their places.

D. The idea that the king would hire foreigners, for pay, to kill his own subjects, struck Americans as a horrific example of cheap despotism; however, the use of mercenaries had a long and distinguished tradition in European warfare, stretching back to the later Middle Ages.

  1. Beginning in the mid-1600s, European armies began recruiting more and more of their armies from their home populations.

  2. But George III brought over into the British service entire regiments of German soldiers, the biggest contingent of which was 17 regiments and a jäger corps from Hesse-Kassel (which is why all the Germans tended to be referred to as "Hessians").

  3. Between August 1775 and February 1776 some 18,000 German troops were signed up for British service.

IV. The king recalled Thomas Gage in September for "consultation" and on October 10 Gage turned over command in Boston to William Howe.

  A. William Howe, like his two older brothers, had had a spectacular military career and had been elected to Parliament for Nottingham in 1758. Nevertheless, he had never had an independent command of his own until now.

  B. The Howe brothers were all Whigs.

  1. William Howe had opposed the Intolerable Acts.

  2. He had assured his Nottingham constituency that he would decline orders to serve in America, though when the orders materialized, he went.

V. The strangest change among the king's servants was in the critical post of secretary of state for the American colonies.

  A. The king nudged aside the Earl of Dartmouth and replaced him on November 10, 1775, with Lord George Sackville Germain, youngest son of the Earl of Dorset.

  1. Like many younger sons, Sackville went into the army.

  2. He rose to lieutenant colonel of the 28th Regiment, commanded the 6th Dragoons, and was elected to Parliament and promoted to major general in 1755.

  3. The smudge on his reputation came when he was court-martialed for failure to obey orders during the Seven Years' War; however, he managed to keep his seat in Parliament.

4. When his widowed aunt died in 1769 he inherited her estate and took her surname.
   5. He worked his way back into the king's good graces by supporting the Stamp Act and all the subsequent Parliamentary legislation for the colonies.
   6. By 1775 he had acquired a reputation for hawkishness in American affairs.
B. Howe and Germain made an odd couple but they agreed entirely on four points.
   1. America was too big to be conquered inch by inch.
   2. Much of America was populated by people still loyal to the king.
   3. It would be vital to strike a blow at the head of the rebellion, either at the rebel army or the rebel Congress.
   4. It would be equally vital to get the Loyalists to take over the work of pulling down the rebel government.
C. They also agreed that Boston was the wrong place to attempt to launch such a blow.
   1. Howe and Germain envisioned abandoning Boston and taking New York City, while a second British army would be built up in Canada.
   2. Both armies could then cut off or crush New England and the southern colonies would learn from this example and return to their ancient loyalty.

Suggested Reading:

Jones, "Sir William Howe," in Billias, *George Washington's Generals and Opponents.*

Mackesy, *The War for America*, chaps. 2–3.

Weintraub, *Iron Tears,* chap. 2.

Questions to Consider:

1. What was the original purpose for recruiting German mercenaries for the American war? How did this become a symbol of British bad faith toward the colonies?

2. What were the major points of the North American strategy developed by Howe and Germain?

Lecture Eight
Conquering Canada, Reconquering Boston

Scope: After the Treaty of Paris in 1763 surrendered all of Canada to Britain, the British managed the French-speaking region quite well thanks to governor-general Sir Guy Carleton. The Americans, however, had a plan to invade and conquer Canada. When Britain's St. John's garrison near the Canadian border surrendered, Carleton lost more than half of the British regulars left in Canada. Benedict Arnold led a second prong of the Canada attack, forcing Carleton to abandon Montreal and almost capturing Quebec. When Burgoyne's British forces arrived, Arnold was forced to retreat to Montreal. But the Americans still had Ticonderoga and the badly needed artillery it provided—artillery that arrived in Boston shortly before the British evacuated the city.

Outline

I. French Canada spread from along the St. Lawrence Riverway and the Great Lakes down to what is now Illinois to touch France's other great North American colony.

   A. France and England had fought a series of ever-escalating wars in Europe and proxy wars in North America that climaxed in the Seven Years' War, which in America became the French and Indian War.

   B. Ultimately, the French had neither the numbers nor the command of the seas necessary to support Canada.

   C. The Treaty of Paris in 1763 surrendered all of Canada to Britain.

   D. Of the 76,000 colonists, or *habitants*, in Canada, only two percent spoke English. Most were French and Catholic at a time when English Protestants were deeply suspicious of Catholicism.

   E. Nonetheless, the British managed French-speaking Canada more adeptly than they had their 13 English-speaking colonies, owing largely to Canada's governor-general, Sir Guy Carleton.

   1. He stood up for their trading rights.
   2. He promoted French-speaking Canadians in public office.
   3. He ignored the prevailing Roman Catholicism of the province.

    4. He lobbied Parliament for the Quebec Act of 1774, confirming Canadian property titles and giving Roman Catholicism legal standing in Canada.

  F. The Quebec Act caused some discontent among the *habitants*.
    1. It imposed the use of English Common Law.
    2. It denied the Canadians a provincial legislature.
    3. It provided for the public support of Protestant churches.

  G. Nevertheless, Carleton was able to send two of the five regiments under his control to reinforce Thomas Gage in Boston.

II. The Continental Congress wanted as many of the North American British provinces in the same boat with it as possible, as well as the West Indies.

  A. In December 1774, the colonial assembly in Jamaica protested the "unrestrained exercise of legislative Power" by Parliament.
    1. The West Indians had a great deal to lose economically by any loss of trade with the 13 colonies.
    2. The white sugar planters of the Caribbean needed the protection of the British army from uprisings by their slaves.

  B. In Canada, however, there was enough discontent among the *habitants* to make the idea of Canada becoming the 14th colony in the Continental Congress look worthwhile.

  C. Arnold laid out a plan to Congress.
    1. The conquest of Canada would add territory and resources to the Congress.
    2. It would prevent the British from using the Hudson River corridor to strike the American army around Boston from behind.

  D. Arnold met with George Washington and Philip Schuyler, who had been appointed to create a "Northern Department" to protect the northern border, to discuss his plan.
    1. Schuyler already had his own plans for a Canadian invasion.
    2. He had three Connecticut regiments and four newly raised New York regiments, and an artillery company, along with Ethan Allen's Green Mountain Boys.
    3. Schuyler also had a talented subordinate, Richard Montgomery, who fumed at Ticonderoga while Schuyler organized his Northern Department.

4. In August, Montgomery bolted up Lake Champlain with about 1,200 men to Fort St. John, where Guy Carleton had posted the 7th and 26th regiments as the first line of defense for Montreal.

E. When Schuyler caught up with Montgomery, he found that Montgomery's raw levies had stumbled into an ambush, launched two inept attacks on Fort St. John, and were on the point of mutiny.
   1. Schuyler left and headed back to Ticonderoga.
   2. Montgomery began a siege of Fort St. John. The ultimate surrender of the St. John's garrison meant a loss of more than half of the British regulars left in Canada.
   3. The road to Montreal was now undefended.

III. Carleton was facing other problems.

A. In August, Washington informed Schuyler of a second prong to the attack on Canada to Quebec via the Kennebec River, with a strike force of 1,000 men under the command of Benedict Arnold. This plan would either force Carleton to allow Schuyler to reach Montreal or to allow Quebec to fall into the Americans' hands.

B. Despite poor planning, unanticipated early frosts, and the sheer forbidding hostility of the Maine woods, Arnold's expedition reached Quebec after 51 days, to the astonishment of Guy Carleton.
   1. With Montgomery now advancing on Montreal and Arnold threatening Quebec, Carleton had only a Hobson's choice before him.
   2. On November 11 he ordered Montreal abandoned and headed for Quebec, narrowly escaping capture by Montgomery's force.

C. If Arnold had struck Quebec at that moment, Canada might well have fallen to the Americans for good because Carleton could only muster 200 men.
   1. Arnold, however, had only managed to bring 550 men up the St. Lawrence, after desertion and hardship had thinned his ranks.
   2. He decided to wait for Montgomery, who did not arrive till December 1, when a nasty winter was setting in, and he brought only 300 men with him.
   3. They tried laying siege to Quebec as they had to Fort St. John.

D. On December 30, they decided on a surprise attack under the cover of a snowstorm.

    1. Arnold fought his way into the lower town from the North, while Montgomery led another 200 men in from the south.

    2. Montgomery was cut down, and his party fell back. And Arnold, also wounded, abandoned the attack.

    3. Arnold fell back into a long encirclement of Quebec that ended on March 4, 1776, when a British relief force under General John Burgoyne arrived and the Americans retreated to Montreal.

E. It was now Carleton's turn to take the offensive.

    1. He forced Arnold from Montreal on June 9, and pursued him all the way to Fort St. John. He stopped there until October, waiting for reinforcements.

    2. When he finally moved his troops onto Lake Champlain, he found Arnold blocking his way with a makeshift fleet of 13 gunboats.

    3. Carleton managed to sink or scuttle the gunboats, but then he pulled back to Canada to wait until the following spring.

F. Ticonderoga still remained securely in American hands.

IV. If Arnold and Montgomery had done nothing else on their Canadian venture than prevent a British descent on Ticonderoga in 1775 and 1776, their effort would have been more than worth it.

A. The nearly 100 pieces of artillery in storage there was what Washington's army around Boston needed more than any other type of weaponry.

B. Artillery on the 18th-century battlefield was the checkmate to the bayonet.

    1. Well-served field guns firing solid iron balls or shotgun-like blasts of grapeshot and canister could break up oncoming formations of attacking infantry better than volleys of musket fire.

    2. The impact was as much psychological as physical.

    3. The troops in an attacking infantry company could see the ball from a 6-pounder coming slowly toward them and know what it would do to them.

C. Washington particularly needed the bigger 18-pounder and 24-pounder guns, short-barreled howitzers, and siege mortars, because these had the range or the high-angle trajectory to reach targets in Boston from his positions.

D. Washington had Henry Knox, a Boston bookseller and civilian engineer, commissioned colonel of his artillery and sent him off to Ticonderoga to retrieve the unwieldy arms.

E. By the time the guns arrived at the end of January, Washington was aware that Howe and the British intended to evacuate Boston as soon as the spring thaws allowed the ships to move in Massachusetts Bay.

    1. On March 4, 1,200 laborers started working on Dorchester Heights, throwing up two redoubts spiked with Knox's artillery.

    2. Howe moved up the evacuation timetable and on March 17, 9,000 British soldiers, their dependents, and more than 1,000 Loyalists left Boston for the last time.

Suggested Reading:

Desjardins, *Through a Howling Wilderness*, chaps. 10–11.

Smith, "Sir Guy Carleton," in Billias, *George Washington's Generals and Opponents*.

Stephenson, *Patriot Battles,* chap. 14.

Questions to Consider:

1. Why did Washington need artillery in order to besiege Boston?

2. How would you contrast the roles played as colonial governors played by Thomas Gage and Guy Carleton?

Lecture Nine
Common Sense

Scope: William Howe and Lord Germain determined that British success in America depended on Howe's ability to destroy Washington's army and seize New York, and on the ability of southern Loyalists to overthrow the rebels. Poor communication, unclear objectives, and the uncertainty of the participation of southern Loyalists, however, jeopardized the plan. Furthermore, British general Clinton tried unsuccessfully to attack Charleston, and British forces found Americans difficult to evict from Canada.

In London, the king had granted the newly appointed commander of the navy in North America, Admiral Lord Richard Howe, and his brother William, powers to negotiate with, as well as fight against, the Americans. Their negotiating powers, however, were never tested. By the time "Black Dick" Howe arrived in America on July 20, 1776, the colonies had already declared themselves free and independent states. Although almost no one had come to the First Continental Congress wanting such a break with Great Britain, the actions of the king and his army had weakened existing ties, and the power of Thomas Paine's *Common Sense* caused the tide to turn toward independence.

Outline

I. George Washington and William Howe could both see that control of the Hudson River Valley would make or break the American rebellion.

    A. By controlling the Hudson, the British could strategically cut the colonies in half.

        1. The southern half would probably then return to the king.

        2. The northern half would be isolated and face a multipointed invasion from New York and Canada.

    B. British success, so envisioned by Lord George Germain and Howe, would depend on two things.

        1. Howe would have to destroy Washington's army and seize New York.

        2. The Loyalists of the southern colonies would have to take an active part, raising their own militias to overthrow the rebels.

C. Believing that the rebellion could be suppressed in one strenuous campaign, Germain arranged substantial reinforcements for Howe, of Hessians, five regiments of elite infantry, and a cavalry regiment.

D. Germain wasted no time in rallying the southern Loyalists.
   1. Assurances that the king's followers would rally if enough British military force were shown came from the deposed royal governor of North Carolina, Josiah Martin.
   2. Maj. Gen. Henry Clinton was detached from Howe's army in January to take command of an expeditionary force to reinforce Loyalist recovery of the southern colonies.
   3. Germain provided Clinton with eight regiments of infantry under major general and Earl Cornwallis and a navy flotilla under Admiral Peter Parker.

E. Germain also sent a relief force for the rescue of Guy Carleton and Quebec—seven infantry regiments and assorted Hessians under Maj. Gen. John Burgoyne. These forces would use the spring and summer of 1776 to secure control of the Hudson River Valley.

F. The plan suffered from three defects.
   1. Organizing, coordinating, and communicating news of these disjointed forces, both to each other and across the ocean to Germain in London was difficult.
   2. The objective of the plan was not unified. Howe had two separate tasks: destroy Washington's army and occupy New York City. It was not clear which he should do first.
   3. The assumption was that the southern colonies contained so many Loyalist apples waiting to fall into their laps.

II. When Henry Clinton finally reached Cape Fear on March 12, he discovered neither Loyalists nor any British troops or British ships were there to greet him.

A. The Parker-Cornwallis fleet did not appear until April and May.

B. Determined to do something, Clinton agreed to attack Charleston.
   1. But Washington had earlier sent his second-in-command, Maj. Charles Lee, to Charleston to supervise the construction of defenses.
   2. By the time Clinton, Cornwallis, and Parker appeared off the harbor mouth in June, there was already a small fort on the tip of Sullivan's Island, which formed the north lip of the harbor.

3. Clinton landed troops north of the fort on June 28, while Parker's ships tried to pound it to pieces.
4. The fort's militia commander, William Moultrie, manned his guns with surprising resourcefulness, and the fort's palmetto-log bulwarks absorbed the British shot instead of splintering and breaking.
5. Clinton finally gave up the whole project.
6. After three weeks he ordered the expedition to head north to join William Howe.

III. In the meantime, Guy Carleton and his reinforcements under Burgoyne were having difficulty evicting the Americans from Canada.

A. It took from June until October 1776 for Carleton and Burgoyne to recover the road south to Lake Champlain; Benedict Arnold's improvised navy at Valcour Island stopped British plans for further campaigning in the Hudson Valley in 1776.

B. Germain and Carleton engaged in quarreling and backbiting, with Germain criticizing the slowness of Carleton's pursuit and confining Carleton to the administration of Canada, leaving offensive operations down the Hudson to Burgoyne.

IV. Germain's appointment was not greeted happily by Parliament, as he was unpopular and considered impractical and ambitious.

A. Whigs complained about the injustice in forcing the Americans into "unconditional submission."

B. Lord North proposed a peace commission for America, an idea that Germain found contemptible.
1. But the newly appointed commander of the navy in North America, Admiral Lord Richard Howe, made it clear that he would not accept his commission unless he and his brother William were granted powers to negotiate with, as well as fight against, the Americans.
2. In May of 1776, the king grudgingly granted the concession, authorizing the Howe brothers to offer pardons to deserving subjects who would return to their allegiance.
3. The Howe brothers were even empowered to offer a political settlement.

V. But when "Black Dick" Howe arrived in America on July 20, it was too late for negotiating. On July 4, the Continental Congress had adopted a resolution declaring the United Colonies free and independent states.

    A. Almost no one—apart from a few of the most radical New Englanders—had come to the First Continental Congress wanting a complete break with Great Britain.

        1. Most thought an overthrow of British authority in America lacked legitimacy.

        2. Many Americans feared that such an overthrow would lead to some new and wholly fearful authority, most likely mob rule.

    B. But the imperial army had cut these arguments to shreds.

        1. The colonies now had a professional army, the instrument of an independent nation, not of a grievance committee.

        2. The various provincial conventions and legislatures began petitioning the Continental Congress for recognition as the legitimate governments of their colonies. The Congress approved them and urged other colonies to set up their own conventions.

        3. In May 1776, the Congress passed a blanket resolution putting all governmental power under the authority of the colonists and ordering the suppression of imperial authority.

VI. The greatest gift England made to American Independence was Thomas Paine.

    A. Uneducated and a failure at corset-making, school-teaching, and tax-collecting, he set out for America with a letter of introduction from Benjamin Franklin.

        1. He was hired as the editor of a failing Philadelphia newspaper, *The Pennsylvania Magazine*.

        2. In short order he boosted circulation to 1,500, denouncing slavery, all proposals for compromise with England, and on January 1776, denouncing the entire principle of royalty in a sensational pamphlet called *Common Sense*.

    B. The legitimacy of self-government came from natural law, Paine argued, drawing on the work of John Locke.

        1. Men were born equal in nature and monarchy was an unhappy historical accident. America needed no human king.

        2. What reason and nature dictated instead was a republic, with a representative assembly and a president to secure freedom.

C. Paine's 77-page pamphlet sold 500,000 copies, making it the single greatest American bestseller before *Uncle Tom's Cabin* in 1852. *Common Sense* turned the tide of American opinion.

    1. On June 7, 1776, Virginia's Richard Henry Lee rose to offer an independence resolution to the Continental Congress.

    2. A committee composed of Benjamin Franklin, John Adams, and Thomas Jefferson was created to write a preface, or Declaration, to the resolution.

    3. Jefferson did most of the writing, and on July 4, the resolution and the declaration were formally adopted.

Suggested Reading:

Gruber, "Richard Lord Howe: Admiral as Peacemaker," in Billias, ed., *George Washington's Generals and Opponents.*

Maier, *American Scripture*, chap. 3.

Rakove, *Beginnings of National Politics*, chaps. 5–6.

Questions to Consider:

1. What was the substance of Thomas Paine's argument against monarchy?

2. On what two factors was British success in 1776 dependent?

Lecture Ten
An Army Falls in Brooklyn

Scope: The optimism of the July 4 declaration was short-lived. Washington's army was poorly manned, poorly supplied, and poorly trained. His officers had little practical experience and what experience they did have varied, so there was no single set of commands with which to train. And some officers such as Charles Lee were more of a hindrance than a help to Washington.

When Admiral Howe arrived in New York in July, he sent to Washington a proclamation stating the proposed peace terms, which Washington refused. What Washington accepted, however, was Charles Lee's assumption that the British would attack the west side of Manhattan in order to force open the Hudson River. Washington and Lee were proven wrong, leading to a disastrous defeat of American forces on Long Island. Only a nor'easter that kept Admiral Howe's ships from cutting off the Americans on Long Island and William Howe's still unexplained decision to halt his pursuit at four in the afternoon on the day of the battle prevented further losses for Continental forces.

Outline

I. Four months after July 4, the heady optimism of the time had evaporated, and the American Revolution looked like it was about to breathe its last breath.

   A. Washington had guessed rightly that Howe's withdrawal from Boston was for the purpose of striking at New York City, so Washington began to take steps toward defending New York.

   B. Two weeks after the British left, Washington himself was on his way to New York to continue strengthening the city's defenses.

   C. Washington's organizing powers had instilled confidence in the army.
   1. He had managed to get rid of most of the troublesome militia units.
   2. In addition to Knox's artillery, Washington had 27 regular Continental regiments with about 14,000 officers and men, plus a reserve of 7,000 militia.

3. By August he had sorted the regiments into five divisions, each of which was formed from a brigade of Continental regiments and a collection of militia.
4. The commanders were Israel Putnam, Maj. Gen. William Heath, Joseph Spencer, John Sullivan, and Nathanael Greene, the officer whom Washington would come to regard as his first and best.

D. Washington knew, however, that there was much less to this army than met the eye.
1. As many as 4,000 Continentals were sick and unfit for duty or else they were doing garrison work at detached points.
2. Only one of the line regiments was anywhere near full strength; most were only slightly over halfway to full recruitment.
3. Supplies of weapons and powder were thin.
4. The recruits could not be taught full-scale battlefield maneuvers without full complements of men and without necessary weaponry.
5. Likewise, officers were getting no experience in practicing battlefield evolutions.
6. To make matters worse, some of the officers had only the sketchiest ideas of drill and maneuver, while others who had experience did not always have the same experience, or work with the same sets of commands, as others.

E. Even the soldiers who had records of service were proving disappointing, starting with Charles Lee.
1. Lee had served in the British army for 16 years, and at the end of the Seven Years' War he wangled an appointment as major general in the army of the king of Poland. He turned up in America asking for Washington's backing for a new military appointment.
2. Former major generals were scarce in North America, and Congress commissioned him.

F. What Lee had to offer in the way of experience was cancelled, Washington soon came to learn, by his insufferable arrogance.
1. In the spring of 1776 Washington sent Lee ahead of the army to New York to oversee the construction of defenses for the city.

2. Lee disregarded the advice from New York's own Committee of Safety about the best places to erect batteries and fortifications, believing the best strategy would be to allow the British ships to crowd into the harbor, where artillery planted on Brooklyn Heights and the tip of Manhattan could sink them like target practice.
3. Lee was also convinced that if the British attempted to land troops on Manhattan, it would probably be on the west side, so he had the west ends of Manhattan's streets barricaded and threw up more artillery emplacements there.
4. He also laid out a new fort in the Highlands to command the Hudson River if the British got through.
5. It was an intelligent and ambitious plan, but it was wrong.

II. When Washington arrived in April with his Continentals, Lee was off to Charleston to quell a Loyalist uprising and stave off Henry Clinton's approach.

A. William Howe was not in New York either. After leaving Boston, Howe had sailed to Halifax, Nova Scotia, to refit, recruit, and rendezvous with the first reinforcements that Germain had sent.
1. The plan was for him to rendezvous in New York with his brother, Admiral Lord Richard Howe, and with Clinton's expedition returning from the Carolinas.
2. Howe and an advance flotilla sailed into the Lower Bay on June 25. The rest of his armada of transports began arriving shortly.
3. Instead of sailing into range of Charles Lee's artillery batteries, Howe made an unopposed landing on Staten Island.
4. In all, Howe would have about 22,000 men.

B. Admiral Howe soon joined his brother arriving on Long Island on July 12.
1. The day after his arrival Admiral Howe issued a proclamation stating the proposed peace terms and sent letters out to the governors of the colonies and to George Washington.
2. Washington agreed to meet with both brothers on July 20, but only to inform them that the Americans were not interested in begging pardons for defending their rights, and that Admiral Howe's offers were better directed to the Congress in Philadelphia.

      3. Admiral Howe did as directed, and a delegation from Congress came to New York and repeated Washington's declaration that Americans had nothing to seek pardon for.

  C. On August 12 the remaining contingents of William Howe's army arrived.

III. Thus began for George Washington four months of unrelieved woe.

  A. Still operating under Charles Lee's assumption that the British would attack the west side of Manhattan in order to force open the Hudson River, he hurried toward the construction of two more forts, Fort Washington and Fort Lee.

  B. But on August 22, Howe offloaded 15,000 of his troops and 40 cannons on the western beaches of Long Island.

  C. At first, Washington thought this was a feint and sent only modest reinforcements to John Sullivan's division posted on Gowanus Heights to cover Brooklyn and Manhattan's rear door facing Long Island.

      1. But no attack on Manhattan materialized, while more British and German troops were seen landing on the west end of Long Island.

      2. Washington gradually stocked Gowanus Heights with individual brigades from his five divisions.

      3. Now his forces were dispersed thinly over more territory than they could hope to defend, and he had sabotaged his own unity of command.

  D. Howe, however, cared less about fooling around with the Hudson River; what he wanted was to destroy Washington's army.

      1. Henry Clinton, the son of a former royal governor of New York, knew the environs of New York better than most of the Americans defending it.

      2. Clinton pressed for using Long Island geography against the Americans: While Cornwallis attacked the American brigades on Gowanus Heights, Clinton would slip past their left flank through the unguarded Jamaica Pass, attack their rear, crushing the rebel army between his division and Cornwallis's.

  E. It all went off better than Howe or Clinton could have hoped.

      1. Clinton captured the Jamaica Pass and rolled into the rear of American forces on Gowanus Heights; American troops on the right flank collapsed and those in the center folded and ran.

2. By evening the defeated Americans had been forced into a perimeter around the village of Brooklyn.

3. The numbers bespoke the disaster: The British forces lost 61 killed and 267 wounded; the Hessians lost only two killed. Washington never got an accurate count of his losses, but he estimated them at between 700 and 1,000 killed, wounded, or captured.

4. More than three-quarters of Washington's losses were men who had simply thrown down their weapons and surrendered, and that included two major generals.

F. A nor'easter that kept Admiral Howe's ships from cutting off the Americans on Long Island entirely and William Howe's decision to halt his pursuit at four in the afternoon of August 27 gave the Americans some time to pull their forces out of the thick of the battle.

IV. Why Howe called a halt to the battle when the three remaining hours of daylight would have allowed him to overrun the Americans in Brooklyn has never been entirely clear.

A. Was it a statement of caution based on the lesson Howe learned at Bunker Hill?

B. Was it part of the brothers' larger peace strategy?

C. Was it more likely because Howe's army was as disorganized by its victory as Washington's was by its defeat?

Suggested Reading:

Randall, *George Washington,* chap. 13.

Schecter, *The Battle for New York*, chaps. 6–9.

Stephenson, *Patriot Battles*, chap. 15.

Questions to Consider:

1. To what extent was the American defeat at Long Island attributable to Charles Lee?

2. Why did William Howe call so hasty an end to his pursuit of Washington's army?

Lecture Eleven
"A Glorious Issue"

Scope: By September 1776, Congress determined that it was better to secure the Continental army than to secure New York City, so Washington began pulling his troops up the island. In mid-September, Continental troops and militia fled when Howe entered the city through Kip's Bay. The city was now occupied by the British, and increased British security snagged American Nathan Hale, who was hung the next day.

Neither the British nor the Americans were without problems. The British had to grapple with the length and fragility of its lines of communication, supply, and recruitment. Washington faced the fact that the one-year enlistments the Congress had imposed on him were soon to expire and Charles Lee continued to be a thorn in his side. Howe then resumed pursuit of Washington's army, forcing it to cross over the Delaware River into Pennsylvania. Tom Paine managed to turn the Americans' resulting despair into hope and inspiration with a new pamphlet, *The American Crisis*. The arrival of reinforcements inspired Washington further to plan a surprise strike on Trenton, which he successfully carried out on December 26, 1776.

Outline

I. Rain throughout the days of August 28 and 29, 1776, kept Admiral Howe's ships out on the East River, giving Washington cover for a pull-out from Brooklyn.

   A. His extraordinary success in pulling 9,500 men from certain siege and capture on Long Island was promptly rewarded by mass desertions by the newly rescued militia.

   B. Washington would probably have preferred abandoning Manhattan altogether, except for his direct order from the Continental Congress to defend New York City.

   C. By mid-September, even the Congress had to agree that securing the army was more important than securing the city.

1. Between September 12 and September 14, Washington began slowly pulling his army back up to Harlem Heights (at the modern-day 124th and 125th streets).
2. Washington also recruited Capt. Nathan Hale to slip into Howe's camps and find out where Howe's next attack would land.

II. William Howe chose this moment to ferry a force of 4,000 across the East River to Kip's Bay, halfway up the east side of Manhattan.

    A. He meant to divide the American line of retreat in half, cutting off all of Washington's army below that line.

    B. The 900 Connecticut militia that Washington had posted to watch Kip's Bay and the north-south post-road broke and fled.
        1. A furious Washington galloped down the post-road, calling up troops from William Heath's division to repel the British landing.
        2. Panic spread from the militia to the Continentals, who also broke and ran, infuriating Washington.

    C. Israel Putnam, who had been left in command of the 3,500 troops still in the city, hurriedly slipped them to safety along the Hudson River, although they had been forced to abandon all of their equipment.

    D. The city was now occupied by the British, who began marking the property of known rebels as default to the king.
        1. Heavy skirmishing went on between the British and the Americans below Harlem Heights on September 16, and on September 21, a fire burned almost one-fourth of the buildings in the city.
        2. The fire gave the occupiers a case of the jitters, and in the increased security measures they seized Nathan Hale on September 21 and hung him the next day. His last words were an approximation of a quotation from Washington's favorite play, Addison's *Cato: A Tragedy*: "I only regret that I have but one life to lose for my country."

III. In mid-October, Howe moved again.

    A. This time he planned to jump back across the East River, landing at Throgs Neck, marching up the Westchester County side of the East River to a point across from the north tip of Manhattan and surprising the Americans from behind.

      1.   This time the British ran into American scouts and pickets.

      2.   Washington had time to cross over from Manhattan and position his army in the path of the British at White Plains.

B.   At the urging of Nathanael Greene, Washington left around 2,000 men to hold Fort Washington. It was the first of several decisions he would come to regret.

      1.   He arrived at White Plains on October 22 with about 13,000 men.

      2.   Until almost the last minute he discounted the importance of Chatterton's Hill, a steep ridge on the other side of the Bronx River that covered a possible escape route and gave British artillery enough elevation to hit the Americans' lines.

      3.   Washington posted six Continental regiments plus two regiments of militia on Chatterton's Hill.

      4.   When Howe pulled up to Washington's positions at White Plains, he attacked Chatterton's Hill with 4,000 British and Hessian soldiers.

      5.   The American militia collapsed, followed by the Continentals, and Washington found his entire position at White Plains untenable.

C.   Once more, Howe and the weather came to the rescue, as a downpour on October 29 brought Howe's army to a halt and Washington used the protection of the storm to slip across the Hudson.

D.   He wanted to abandon Fort Washington as well, but was talked out of it by Nathanael Greene.

E.   On November 15, Howe gained possession of Fort Washington and summoned the garrison to surrender. Four days later, Fort Lee, across the Hudson, was abandoned to Cornwallis and 4,000 British regulars.

IV. The great dilemma of the British army in this war was the length and fragility of its lines of communication, supply, and recruitment.

    A.   British strategy rested on the assumption that the bulk of the fighting in America was better done by American Loyalists.

    B.   Capt. Johann Ewald, an officer of a Hessian jäger unit, also thought that Howe did not want to inflict so great a humiliation on the Americans that they would resort to partisan or guerilla warfare.

V. Washington faced some daunting problems as well.

    A. The short one-year enlistments that the Congress had imposed on him in Boston were beginning to run out and would reduce his army to 7,500 in a few weeks.

    B. Charles Lee, who Washington put at the head of a contingent of 2,000 New Jersey Continentals, continued to be a thorn in his side.

    C. On December 1, Washington learned that General Howe had resumed pursuit, and Washington ordered a retreat to the Raritan River in northern New Jersey.

        1. By the time they reached Princeton, Washington's army was down to 3,700 men, and Lee was inventing excuses for his Continentals not to join them.

        2. On December 7 the last fragments of Washington's Continental army crossed over the Delaware River and into Pennsylvania.

        3. In November, the Howe brothers issued an amnesty proclamation, and over 3,000 Americans flocked to swear allegiance to the king and to receive papers guaranteeing their lives and property.

        4. Congress fled Philadelphia for Baltimore.

VI. Traveling with Washington's army on the retreat through New Jersey was Thomas Paine.

    A. The repeated defeats, the fading numbers, and the depleted morale of the Continental army fired his temper, and by the time the Delaware was reached, he had written *The American Crisis.*

        1. "These are the times that try men's souls," the pamphlet began famously.

        2. Paine pointed out that the retreat had been orderly and the American forces had showed no fear.

    B. Within a day, *The American Crisis* was circulating through the army and spirits were lifting.

VII. The British did Washington another favor when a squadron of the 17th Dragoons crept up on the headquarters of Charles Lee, captured him, and carried him off to New York.

    A. Within a few days, Lee's replacement, John Sullivan, brought Lee's 2,000 Continentals into Washington's camp and 600 New Hampshire militia arrived from Ticonderoga. These additions brought Washington's numbers up to 7,600.

B. On December 13, Howe proposed to call off further military operations for the winter, another "gift" for Washington.

C. With the arrival of his reinforcements, however, Washington had begun planning a surprise strike at Trenton, where a Hessian brigade had been stationed.

    1. On Christmas night, using the storm as cover, Washington attempted to cross over the ice-choked Delaware with 2,400 Continentals, while 800 Pennsylvania militia would cross just below the town and seize the exit road.

    2. Only some of the men managed to get across, but that was more than enough. On the morning of December 26, they hit Trenton fiercely, and the Hessians surrendered.

D. But the greatest capture Washington achieved at Trenton was the initiative.

Suggested Reading:

Fischer, *Washington's Crossing*, chaps. 12–14.

Schecter, *Battle for New York,* chaps. 10, 12–17.

Stephenson, *Patriot Battles,* chap. 16.

Questions to Consider:

1. Why did Paine's *American Crisis* have such a mesmerizing effect on American morale?

2. Why did Washington wait until the end of December to launch a counter-stroke at the British?

Lecture Twelve
Joy in Princeton

Scope: Despite the victory at Trenton, Washington still had to convince his soldiers to reenlist. After a touching appeal by Washington, 1,200 of his men reenlisted, giving him a total of 3,300 Continentals. Several militia units turned up as well. A second Battle of Trenton and a strike at Princeton were also successful for Americans in early 1777. No battles were fought for three months thereafter, so Washington took this time to reorganize his army, deciding first that militia would be used only for garrison and reserves and second, that the brigade, not the regiment, was the most effective tactical unit.

Lord Germain had prophesied that New Jersey was a colony that would produce a wellspring of Loyalists. After Trenton, however, those Loyalists were badly shaken. With the king's army gone, the king's victims were looking for revenge, not just on Loyalists but on any fence-sitters as well, and many had to leave their homes. New Jersey Loyalist slaves, however, did not mind leaving their homes and many happily ran for freedom.

Outline

I. Washington's surprise at Trenton threw the British occupation of New Jersey into a panic and moved Carl von Donop, who was in overall command of the outposts at Trenton, Burlington, and Bordentown, to order a pullback to Princeton.

   A. Washington's instincts were to keep von Donop retreating.

   B. A council of his officers, however, pointing to the bad weather, the number of prisoners, and the pitiful condition of the men, advised a retreat to safety back in Pennsylvania.

   C. Short-term enlistments were also going to run out on December 31.
      1. Washington implored the Philadelphia financier Robert Morris to obtain enough hard cash to offer a $10 bounty to every man who would reenlist.
      2. He paraded Greene's and Sullivan's divisions to make a personal appeal, to no effect.

3. Then he made a second appeal, one of his rare moments of forceful eloquence, and the men in the ranks began to waver, and by ones and twos, then by companies, they stepped forward, until 1,200 men had volunteered.

II. All told, Washington managed to hold on to about 3,300 Continentals.

   A. The militia now decided to come to Washington's aid as well.

      1. These militias were untrained, undisciplined, and spoiling to avenge themselves on Loyalists who had fingered them to the British.

      2. But they were there, and if Washington did not use them, they could just as easily melt away again.

   B. Washington called a council of war and persuaded his officers to strike at von Donop in Princeton. He needed to move quickly because the British were not sitting idle.

      1. Earl Cornwallis had taken personal command of the scattered forces left in New Jersey.

      2. Cornwallis collected two brigades-worth of troops (including von Donop's Hessians) and set off for Trenton where they met the Continentals who held them back.

      3. By evening, Washington estimated that Cornwallis had lost 500 killed and wounded.

   C. But Washington knew that Cornwallis would begin looking for a way to cross the creek in order to pin the Americans against the Delaware.

      1. Instead of waiting for the attack, Washington pulled his army back over the creek under cover of night, swung south and east, and arrived at Cornwallis's rear.

      2. Cornwallis's men were just waking at Trenton when they were surprised by the sound of heavy cannon in their rear.

   D. British Lt. Col. Charles Mawhood had spied advance elements of Washington's men coming northward on Quaker Road.

      1. Mawhood decided to attack. His men hit Nathanael Greene's men in the middle of an apple orchard just off the Quaker Road.

      2. Mawhood's men were outnumbered nearly three to one, but the regulars stood their ground and advanced with the bayonet.

      3. But there were more Americans coming up, and the 17th Regiment finally retreated and then fought its way back to Cornwallis.

    4. The 55th Regiment was surrounded at Princeton by Sullivan's division and surrendered.

    5. The 40th Regiment was battered into submission by American artillery under young Alexander Hamilton.

    6. Mawhood's force lost almost half its numbers: 222 killed and wounded out of 446 men.

E. Washington took little joy from this victory. His goal had been the great British supply depot at New Brunswick, and Mawhood's resistance had cost him the entire day and allowed Cornwallis to get his own troops moving in pursuit.

F. Washington now swerved north toward the Watchung Mountains of northern New Jersey and an encampment at Morristown.

    1. But Howe was unwilling to take any more chances and ordered a general retreat to Perth Amboy.

    2. The next three months would see skirmishes and ambushes all across New Jersey but no major battles.

III. Morristown was a settlement with a population of between 250 and 300 people and some 50 or 60 buildings that had to accommodate the tired, hungry, and ill-clothed Continentals.

A. Some Continentals could be lodged in various structures, but the rest had to build log huts in the snow, and some froze to death.

B. Only 800 of the $10 bounty men permanently reenlisted.

C. Smallpox swept through the camp, forcing Washington to decree mandatory inoculations.

IV. During this time, Washington experimented with a dramatic reorganization of the army.

A. His experience of the last year had led him to two important conclusions.

    1. The militia was useful for nothing but reserve and garrison duties, and Congress would have to pay for a full-fledged professional army.

    2. The brigade, not the regiment, was the most effective tactical unit.

B. Reorganizing an army, however, only works if there is a real army to reorganize.

    1. While the new Continental regiments were enlisted, Washington could not afford to have the militias go home.

2. He did not want the new Continental army to be filled with riff-raff, and he charged those who were recruiting officers to take only gentlemen.

V. New Jersey's Loyalists were caught between a rock and a hard place.

    A. New Jersey had seemed to be most likely to fulfill Lord George Germain's prophecy that the Loyalist sympathy would rise up and end the Revolution.

        1. William Howe began appointing recruitment and got 850 Loyalists by November.

        2. This lasted until exactly after Trenton; once the British began their retreat back to their Raritan River enclave, the Loyalists and the families of recruits began looking for reassurance from their neighbors that their Loyalist enthusiasm would not be held against them.

        3. That reassurance was not forthcoming.

        4. Howe's regulars had been kept pretty well in hand, but the same could not be said of the Hessians, for whom plunder was a means of improving one's income.

    B. Now the king's army was gone and the king's victims were eager for revenge, so the New Jersey Loyalists found themselves in danger.

        1. Washington issued a proclamation demanding that anyone who had signed the king's oath surrender and take the oath of allegiance to the United States of America within 30 days.

        2. But even those who had not taken the king's oath, but who had only tried to keep their heads down, were not exempt from harassment and threats.

    C. One group of Loyalists that had no difficulty about fleeing was New Jersey's black slaves.

        1. The calling out of the militia and the back-and-forth of the armies had created an atmosphere of instability which, of itself, loosened the bonds of slavery.

        2. Once the British army moved into New Jersey, slaves in Monmouth ran off and boarded the British ships in New York harbor.

        3. In February there were enough slaves behind British lines to form a regiment of Black Pioneers and Guides, organized as a field engineer battalion.

4. Titus Corlies, a Monmouth County slave, organized a partisan unit of black Loyalists that specialized in scouting, raids, barn-burnings, and ambushes of rebel New Jerseyans.

Suggested Reading:

Fischer, *Washington's Crossing*, chaps. 16–17.

Stephenson, *Patriot Battles,* chap. 10.

Wright, *The Continental Army,* chap. 5.

Questions to Consider:

1. What motivated Americans to volunteer for service with the Loyalist militia?

2. What were the most important elements of Washington's reorganization of the army at Morristown?

Lecture Thirteen
"Congress Are Not a Fit Body"

Scope: In early March 1777, the Continental Congress returned to
Philadelphia after a tedious spell of inactivity in Baltimore, where
it had fled the British advance to the Delaware River. The
delegates were facing tasks they had never experienced before,
such as the establishment, outfitting, and management of an army.
Congress tried to pass much of this responsibility onto the states,
but the states had their own militia to support. Congress's solution
was to create myriad committees to carry out myriad functions,
both executive and legislative. However, there weren't enough
people in Congress to carry out both legislative and executive
functions. After all, the Congress was an ad hoc body with no legal
standing to govern the states and with no power to levy taxes. In
addition, states were suspicious of the Congress's attempts to
control them and to form any kind of a union. Unable to solve
these challenges, the Congressional delegates were disposed to
blame the costly, dangerous army—and Washington. And they
also managed to take steps to form an alliance with France.

Outline

I.   In March 1777, the Continental Congress returned to Philadelphia from
     Baltimore, where it had fled the British advance to the Delaware River.

   A. The delegates vested broad powers in General Washington and left
        for Baltimore.

   B. In Baltimore, by mid-January, the number of congressional
        delegates had dwindled considerably.
        1. Of the 345 members who served in the Second Continental
             Congress from May 1775 until its final adjournment in 1788,
             not more than 65 had met together at one time in the first two
             years of the war. In time to come, that number would drop as
             low as nine.
        2. The turnover rate among the membership at large was not
             encouraging either.

II. These delegates were also facing tasks that none of them had ever faced before.

    A. Those who had served in the colonial legislatures had argued with royal governors, voted taxes for various public works, and appointed a handful of colonial offices.

    B. They were wholly unprepared for what awaited them as members of the Continental Congress, and that was especially true of the affairs of the Continental army.

        1. They had been called upon to authorize the creation of an army and all it entailed and then finding some way to pay for it all.

        2. Congress coped by forming committees: 114 in 1777 alone, and 3,429 during the course of the war.

    C. Congress's first instinct had been to lay as much of the war-making responsibility onto the states as it could.

        1. But the states had militias of their own to outfit, so Congress resorted to creating the committees to do these jobs itself, starting in September 1775, with a Secret Committee responsible for arming and equipping the Continental army.

        2. This move soon necessitated the creation of myriad other committees to handle such issues as import agreements, warfare at sea, the Continental treasury, and medical affairs.

    D. The reality was that the Continental Congress was first a legislative body, but the war forced it to take on executive functions as well.

        1. No one really had time or expertise for both functions, but no one was willing to give up being both.

        2. But the Congress had become obsessed with concentrating power in its hands alone.

III. The Continental Congress suffered from two major structural defects that kept it from exercising the power it was intent on holding.

    A. First, it was an ad hoc body that had no legal standing.

    B. Second, it had no power to levy taxes directly on the people of the states or on the states themselves.

        1. Congress had no assets of its own.

        2. It could raise money only by borrowing at home or abroad, or by printing it in the form of promissory notes, paper currency and "quartermaster's certificates" in lieu of hard coin to contractors and soldiers.

IV. The failure to find some independent means of funding the Congress produced a nightmare.

    A. Army officers who were Continental quartermasters often tapped their own funds and credit to feed and equip their troops.

    B. By 1779 the army was £2 million in debt and mistrust of army credit was widespread.

    C. Congress hoped that printing its own unsecured paper currency would persuade farmers and merchants to part more readily with supplies, but the unsecured Continental bills only drove prices up and created a black market for operating in hard coin.

V. The primary object of the colonial rebellion had been to throw off the British yoke.

    A. In many places the vacuum created by the annihilation of British rule was filled by replacing them with Americanized elites.

    B. In other states, the crowds in the streets were determined to prevent the substitution of one unpopular government for another unpopular government. These states became laboratories for experiments in republican politics.

        1. In Pennsylvania, the office of governor was eliminated as "too monarchical" and replaced with an executive committee and a single-house assembly elected through broadly democratized voting rights.

        2. Twelve of the new revolutionary governors rose from the lowest ranks of colonial society.

    C. If the states were so disinclined to trust the "great men" within their own boundaries, they could not be expected to be any less resentful at the attempts of an alien Congress to control them.

        1. The first call for a "plan of union" was offered in Congress by Richard Henry Lee as part of the same resolution that triggered the Declaration of Independence.

        2. A committee formed in June 1776 and led by John Dickinson produced a draft set of "articles of confederation" clearly aimed at refashioning Congress into a national government with exclusive and sovereign powers over the states.

        3. Suspicions of the states, and between the states, kept the Articles of Confederation stalled in Congress until the end of 1777, and unratified by the requisite number of states until 1781.

VI. None of this boded well for George Washington in the winter of 1776–1777.

    A. Expenses and conflicts were mounting because the war was dragging on, and many thought the war was dragging on because the wrong people were fighting it.

        1. A standing professional army such as Washington promoted was the bête noire of every republican political theorist.

        2. Therefore, it was easy to blame the Continental Congress's frustrations on Washington's Continental army.

    B. It was also easy to blame Washington himself.

        1. Congress saw Washington as a would-be Caesar—except that he routinely lost battles.

        2. John Adams was suspicious of the way members of Congress "idolized" Washington.

        3. Congress created new headaches for Washington by foisting on him a string of European military officers with dubious records.

VII. There was one thing the Congress did manage to do right, and that was to take steps to form an alliance with France.

    A. For years, Louis XV had wanted a rematch of the war which had cost him pride and his American possessions, and his successor, Louis XVI, and his advisor, the Comte de Vergennes, believed that the weakest link in Britain's chain of empire was the American colonies.

    B. But the Congress and the Continental army would have to prove that it could do more than merely avoid defeat before France would take any risks.

Suggested Reading:

Buchanan, *The Road to Valley Forge*, chaps. 10–11.

Carp, *To Starve the Army at Pleasure*, chaps. 1–3.

Rakove, *The Beginnings of National Politics*, chaps. 7–9.

Questions to Consider:

1. What factors crippled the ability of the Continental Congress to function effectively?

2. In what ways was the Continental Congress more of a hindrance than a help to Washington and the Continental army?

Lecture Fourteen
"America Is Not Subdued"

Scope: Trenton and Princeton broke the happy bubble of self-congratulation in which Lord George Germain had ended the year 1776. Parliament did not welcome the reassessment of what would be needed to win the war, but the Whig opposition was too weak to slow the king or Lord North's government. Maj. Gen. John Burgoyne presented to Lord George Germain a plan for invading from Canada with two strike forces. Sir William Howe would then bring his army north to rendezvous with Burgoyne at Albany, and they would jointly subdue New England. Germain happily put Burgoyne in command. The forces were far short of Burgoyne's request, but he managed to retake Ticonderoga before he was stalled by his supply train's slow progress. Philip Schuyler, preparing to block Burgoyne's progress to Albany, was recalled by Congress and replaced by his second in command, Horatio Gates. Burgoyne slowly got his army to Fort Edward, where he learned that Howe would not be joining him at Albany.

Outline

I. Lord George Germain ended the year 1776 exultant.

    A. His insistence that aggressive war was the only acceptable response to the uproar in America had all the appearance of working.

        1. The Northern army was in retreat.

        2. Loyalists were renewing their allegiance to the king and began shouldering the responsibility for suppressing the rebellion.

        3. General Howe had grown so confident that the end was near that he had peeled off part of his army under Henry Clinton and sent it off to a successful invasion and occupation of Newport, Rhode Island.

        4. In Parliament, Lord Germain introduced a bill to expedite the arrests of the Americans by suspending the operation of the writ of *habeas corpus* in the colonies.

B. This happy bubble burst on the news of Trenton and Princeton.

    1. Through most of 1776, the Whig opposition had given up on opposing the king's demand for war, but the news of Trenton and the *habeas corpus* bill brought them back.

    2. Still, the *habeas corpus* bill passed by 195 to 43.

II. Maj. Gen. John Burgoyne landed in England on December 9, 1776, and met with Lord Germain the next day to propose a plan of his own for the reconquest of America.

  A. "Gentlemanly Johnny" Burgoyne has come down in historical reputation as an arrogant incompetent with a total lack of military sense, which is surely about 90 percent untrue.

    1. Young Burgoyne joined as a junior officer in the 13th Light Dragoons in 1740, and in due course promotion opened up for him.

    2. In the Seven Years' War, he demonstrated aptitude for command, and he rose to lieutenant colonel of the 11th Dragoons in 1759, and was commissioned to raise a new regiment of light dragoons, the 16th, which became known as "Burgoyne's Light Horse."

    3. In 1761 he won a seat in Parliament, where, in 1774, he urged the North government to use persuasion rather than force.

  B. The English aristocracy regarded him as a mannerless *parvenu*.

    1. When in 1775 it was clear that the North government was planning a military solution in America, he changed his views and put himself forward for seconding to America with Howe and Clinton.

    2. He was hardly on the ground in Boston before he began advertising plans of his own for ending the standoff and wrote letters denigrating Gage, Howe, Clinton, and Carleton.

  C. Complaints about Carleton were music to the ears of Lord Germain.

    1. Germain and Carleton had already had run-ins.

    2. After the defeats at Trenton and Princeton, Germain was ready to hear from a general with plans to do what Carleton had not done.

III. On February 28, 1777, Burgoyne laid before Germain a series of "Thoughts for Conducting the War from the Side of Canada."

    A. The plan was to finish the job Carleton had abandoned the previous fall, with a few added strategies designed ultimately to crush the heart of the rebellion by subduing New England.

    B. Once New England was subdued, the Loyalists of the southern colonies would return with the tide and everyone would resume loyalty to the king.

    C. Germain put Burgoyne in command and informed Carleton that he was henceforth to concern himself with Canadian affairs only.

    D. As Burgoyne left London, he realized at the last minute that he had failed to communicate at all with William Howe and dashed off a note from shipboard.

    E. When Burgoyne arrived at Quebec in May 1777, and presented his orders to Sir Guy Carleton, the governor-general complied.

IV. "Gentlemanly Johnny" marshaled his forces with surprising speed, but from the beginning, two shadows fell across his path.

    A. The first was numbers. Burgoyne would have to make do with a top strength of 7,300; far fewer than he had requested in London.

    B. The second shadow was one that Burgoyne would discover much later—too late, in fact.

    C. Shorthanded as he was, Burgoyne set out southward toward Lake Champlain and easily dislodged American rebels from Fort Ticonderoga.

    D. But now the landscape began to tell on Burgoyne. After 18 days he was only three miles below Ticonderoga, owing to the laggardliness of his artillery-heavy supply train.

V. Meanwhile Philip Schuyler and his Northern army destroyed whatever roads and bridges the British might try to use.

    A. He had about 3,000 Continentals under his command and perhaps as many as 1,500 militia, and he warned the Congress that unless he got more, he would be forced to retreat further.

    B. The Congress's response was to send Schuyler orders to report in person to Washington, preparatory to a court-martial, and turn his department over to Horatio Gates.

1. Gates had originally been seconded by Washington to the Northern Department to assist Schuyler, but the two had quarreled over authority, and in the spring of 1777 Gates had a choice of either submitting to Schuyler or going back to his old job with Washington.

2. Instead, he went to Congress and denounced Schuyler.

C. This should have cost Gates his credibility, but as Schuyler's reputation sank, Gates looked better and better, and by August, Gates was in charge of Schuyler's department.

D. Washington sent him what reinforcements he could spare, including Benjamin Lincoln of Massachusetts and Benedict Arnold.

VI. Burgoyne did not get his army moving until July 24, and then it took 10 days to travel the 16 miles overland to Fort Edward, where the second shadow fell across his path.

A. A letter from William Howe, written on July 17, informed Burgoyne that instead of joining him at Albany, William Howe had put his entire force on transports and was sailing to the Chesapeake Bay.

B. Burgoyne was utterly on his own, with no good choices.

Suggested Reading:

Furneaux, *Saratoga*, chaps. 4–6.

Ketchum, *Saratoga*, chaps. 15–18.

Pancake, *1777: The Year of the Hangman*, chaps. 6, 8.

Stephenson, *Patriot Battles*, chap. 18.

Questions to Consider:

1. Why did Germain and Burgoyne believe that a Hudson Valley strategy would bring the Revolution to a close?

2. Why was Horatio Gates selected for command of the Northern army?

Lecture Fifteen
"A Day Famous in the Annals of America"

Scope: "Gentleman Johnny" Burgoyne devised a plan to secure supplies by sending some units to Bennington, Vermont, where there was reportedly a storehouse of food and horses. Burgoyne was unaware that militia companies from New York and all over New England were converging on Bennington under John Stark. Despite losing the battles that ensued, Burgoyne decided to push on to Albany, unaware that Horatio Gates was on his way north with 10,000 Continentals and militia. Burgoyne met the first elements of Gates's army near Stillwater. His unsuccessful attacks on Bemis Heights, where Gates's forces were securely entrenched, cost him heavy losses. Assistance from Sir Henry Clinton was too little, too late. After Benedict Arnold successfully fought off one more of Burgoyne's attempts at Bemis Heights, Burgoyne retreated and surrendered. This shattering news energized Parliamentary opposition to the war, but the king was obdurate. Then came more bad news: The Americans had signed a treaty with the French.

Outline

I. The deeper Burgoyne moved into the forests, the more conditions deteriorated and supplies dwindled.

    A. The day after receiving Howe's letter announcing his departure for the Chesapeake Bay, Burgoyne came up with a plan.

        1. He wished to send Lt. Col. Friedrich Baum and his dismounted Brunswick dragoons, along with various other units and equipment, to the town of Bennington to seize a storehouse.

        2. If possible, Burgoyne wanted Baum to move south, recruiting Loyalist militia as he went, and rendezvous with Burgoyne at Albany.

    B. Baum had no idea that at almost the same moment, Philip Schuyler's appeals for militia support were drawing in militia companies from nearby states and concentrating them at Bennington, under the command of John Stark.

1. On the morning of August 14, Baum's skirmishers cleared out some rebel militia at a grist mill nine miles west of Bennington.
2. The militia were Stark's skirmishers, and when Baum set off the next morning he was met by more than 1,000 rebel militia.
3. Stark divided his militia regiments into three pincer-like columns that surrounded Baum.
4. Those who fought were cut down, including Baum, while the rest surrendered.

II. The debacle at Bennington was an appalling shock to Burgoyne.
   A. Food was running out and discipline was beginning to deteriorate.
      1. Burgoyne's Mohawk allies quit in disgust.
      2. Even the civilian Canadian teamsters were stealing horses from Burgoyne's dwindling supply of draft animals.
   B. Burgoyne again pondered his alternatives and decided to proceed to Albany.
   C. He stockpiled enough food for 30 days and on September 13 he crossed the Hudson to the Albany side, just below Saratoga, New York.
   D. He appears to have had no idea that Philip Schuyler had by now been replaced by Horatio Gates as commander of the Northern Department.
   E. By the time Burgoyne was preparing to cross the Hudson, Gates had 10,000 Continentals and militia on hand, and on September 7, 1777, Gates put them on the road north.

III. Burgoyne finished his crossing on September 15, and the next day turned southward toward Stillwater, on the Hudson.
   A. Three miles north of Stillwater he collided with the first elements of Gates' army.
      1. A Polish-born military engineer named Thaddeus Kosciuszko had laid out a massive redoubt along Bemis Heights, and Gates had filled it with Continentals on both right and left.
      2. This was not a position Burgoyne wanted to attack head on, but the road beside the river was the only reasonable route to Albany.

B. Burgoyne's grand assault on Bemis Heights began at 10 in the morning on September 19.

    1. Benedict Arnold, one of Gates's Northern Department officers, had guessed what Burgoyne was likely to do, and Burgoyne's attack plans swiftly went awry.

    2. By 4 pm Burgoyne was able to disengage and count his losses: 160 killed, 364 wounded, and 42 missing.

C. On the morning of September 21, an offer of assistance came from Sir Henry Clinton to bring in 2,000 men in about 10 days.

    1. Clinton did not get moving until October 3, and he understood his object as merely providing a diversion, not rescuing Burgoyne.

    2. He attacked some of the American outposts in the Hudson Highlands, and then returned to New York.

D. On October 7, Burgoyne, increasingly desperate, made another unsuccessful attempt on Bemis Heights, during which a British bullet smashed through Benedict Arnold's leg.

E. Now Burgoyne had no choice but to run.

    1. On October 9 he pulled away from his entrenchments, struggling to get safely over the Hudson again.

    2. His men were starving and those who were not starving were deserting.

    3. On the night of October 12 John Stark and his men crossed the Hudson in front of Burgoyne, closing his hope of escape across the Hudson.

F. Burgoyne concluded that there was no way out of the box the Americans had closed around them.

    1. After dickering through intermediaries, Burgoyne and Gates finally reached a settlement.

    2. On October 17, 1777, "Gentlemanly Johnny" surrendered himself, his sword, and 5,900 men.

IV. Three weeks later, news of Burgoyne's surrender arrived in England; the king was *not* happy.

    A. In the House of Commons, Lord Germain was greeted with a blast of denunciation from the opposition benches.

    B. Lord North begged the king to allow him to prepare peace proposals to offer to the Americans or else allow him to resign, but George III refused to part with either North or Germain.

V. Then news arrived that the Americans had signed a treaty with the French. There would now be a war with France as well.

    A. France was more than merely curious about the possibility of joining the American colonies as an ally, but the French were unwilling to embrace the Americans publicly until two conditions were satisfied.

        1. First, the American states had to show that they were united.

        2. Second, they had to show in some dramatic way that they could do more militarily than merely avoid defeat.

    B. In September 1776 the Congress authorized sending John Adams, Silas Deane, and Benjamin Franklin to represent the American cause directly to the French.

        1. Adams was the Congress's best and brightest representative.

        2. Franklin's inclusion demonstrated that even the Congress had to recognize that he was the most famous American in the world.

    C. The tidings of Saratoga were the last push: The Americans had not only defeated, but wiped off the map, an entire British field army.

    D. On February 6, 1778, the commissioners were at last able to sign two formal treaties with France, establishing commercial relations and creating a diplomatic alliance.

Suggested Reading:

Furneaux, *Saratoga*, chaps. 10, 13–14.

Ketchum, *Saratoga*, chaps. 19–21.

Pancake, *1777: The Year of the Hangman*, chaps. 9–10.

Questions to Consider:

1. What role did Benedict Arnold play at Saratoga?

2. Was Saratoga more important as a military victory or a diplomatic one?

Lecture Sixteen
"Not Yet the Air of Soldiers"

Scope: Choosing not to wait for the many months it could take for Lord
Germain to respond to any proposed plans, General Howe acted on
his own initiative and in July 1777, sailed south with his army
from Staten Island, intent on traveling as far up the Chesapeake as
he could, to reach Philadelphia. They found Washington and
nearly 10,000 Continental infantry blocking their road to
Philadelphia at the Brandywine River. The British managed to
break the Americans' fierce resistance at Brandywine, a defeat
witnessed by the young Marquis de Lafayette, whom Washington
had met in Philadelphia. Howe then paused again. Such a delay
prompted Washington to attack, but a heavy rainstorm made
fighting impossible. As Howe continued on toward Philadelphia,
Washington sent four divisions to strike a blow, but Howe struck
first, resulting in the Paoli Massacre. This disaster was followed by
another failed attempt on the British at Germantown.

Outline

I. The rounds of finger-pointing that followed "Gentlemanly Johnny"
Burgoyne's disaster at Saratoga eventually swiveled around to two
people, Lord George Germain and Sir William Howe.

   A. Germain's political enemies hatched the story that Germain had
   neglected to send Howe any notice or direction concerning
   Burgoyne's expedition—a story that was false.

   B. The real culprit, then, was Sir William Howe, who had abandoned
   Burgoyne to his fate in the wilderness for one of two reasons.

      1. Out of pique that Burgoyne was being personally directed by
      Germain, instead of being subordinate to Howe as commander
      in chief in North America.

      2. Because Howe suffered from some kind of psychological
      fixation on completing the campaign that Washington had
      frustrated at the end of 1776.

      3. Neither of these stories was true either.

C. The real problem was the Atlantic Ocean and the three months it could require to cross it.

    1. Howe's campaign plans, written in January 1777, would not return with an approval from Germain until late May or early June.

    2. If Germain's response needed to be clarified, it would take another six months for Howe to get an answer.

D. This was why Howe was commander in chief; he was expected to act on his own initiative, and he did.

    1. Howe assumed that nothing about Burgoyne's orders precluded Howe from embarking on his own campaign to deal with Washington, and dealing with Washington might have been the best way to assist Burgoyne.

    2. In the absence of any rapid way to communicate, Howe, Burgoyne, and Germain were left with the impression that they all understood each other, until it was too late.

    3. They were all guilty of disregarding one of the primary principles of war: unity of command.

II. George Washington had become convinced by the first week of March that Howe intended to move southward again toward Philadelphia.

A. He was puzzled by Howe's movements and by reports that Howe had assembled a fleet of 20 transports in New York harbor.

    1. He concluded that Howe must be planning a severe blow.

    2. Howe was only testing the waters to see if Washington would meet him in an open fight, something Washington wanted to avoid.

B. By July 23, Howe's army had boarded transports and sailed out to sea.

III. On July 30, Howe's fleet was sighted at the mouth of the Delaware Bay, so Washington got his army onto the roads to meet him.

A. He had two divisions of some 15,000 men to manage.

B. This vast machine did not reach the Brandywine River, halfway to Philadelphia, until September 11.

C. When it did it found Washington and fewer than 10,000 Continental infantry drawn up on advantageous ground behind the Brandywine.

    1. Washington had moved his army with remarkable speed.

2. He had galloped ahead to arrive in Philadelphia on August 5, and the army paraded through Philadelphia to the delight of the Congress on August 24.

D. While in Philadelphia, Washington was first introduced to Marie-Joseph-Paul-Yves-Roch Gilbert, the Marquis de Lafayette, a 19-year-old from a rich, noble French family.
   1. He had just arrived from France and was a passionate admirer of the American cause.
   2. Lafayette disarmed Washington by stating at once that he would serve without pay, and if desired, without rank, "as a volunteer."
   3. Washington invited him to join the army on its march down the Brandywine.

IV. Washington reached the Brandywine on September 9, and spread his five divisions on both sides of the main road to Philadelphia.

   A. Sir William Howe saw no reason to depart from the plan which had succeeded so well at Long Island, and on the morning of the eleventh he split his divisions.
      1. One, under Hessian general Knyphausen, to attack straight across the Brandywine at Chadd's Ford.
      2. The other, under Cornwallis, would swing northward and then come down behind Washington's right flank.

   B. It took Knyphausen until 4 pm to cross the Brandywine.
      1. By then, Howe and Cornwallis had crossed the forks of the Brandywine and were advancing toward Washington's rear.
      2. The American lines collapsed, but they held long enough to leave the British very weary by nightfall.
      3. The British had suffered only 89 dead and another 400 or so wounded, while Washington lost 200 dead and another 400 wounded, including Lafayette.

   C. There Howe stopped for two days, sending out only flanking parties to secure communication with the ships of his brother, "Black Dick."
      1. On the fifteenth, Washington recrossed the Schuylkill and deployed along the Lancaster Pike on the flank of the British advance.
      2. Before the two armies could engage again a thunderous rainstorm descended on them, making more than isolated skirmishing impossible.

3. After the storm, Howe's army resumed its slow crawl toward Philadelphia.

D. Washington, unsure whether he would have another chance to stop Howe, sent Alexander Hamilton to Philadelphia with a letter advising Congress to evacuate, which they did, to York, Pennsylvania.
   1. On September 19, Washington began sliding Anthony Wayne and his division around the left flank of Howe's advance.
   2. Washington planned to hit Howe head on and then allow Wayne to drive into Howe's flank and rear.
   3. But on the night of September 20, Howe struck first and overran Wayne's encampment using only the bayonet.
   4. Fifty-three of Wayne's men were stabbed or hacked to death; another 220 were wounded or missing.

V. The Paoli Massacre deranged Washington's plans for attacking Howe's army, and on September 26, Cornwallis staged a triumphal entry into Philadelphia.

A. Howe then made the same mistake he had made before Trenton.

B. Washington was joined at Germantown by Alexander McDougall's brigade of Continentals and some militia.

C. He formed four attack columns.
   1. One would move down the Germantown Pike and hit the British outposts just outside Germantown.
   2. A second would smash into the British right flank.
   3. A third would slip behind that flank and cut off any British retreat toward Philadelphia.
   4. A fourth would surprise the Hessian jäger outposts between the village and the river.
   5. As if to replicate the conditions at Trenton, a thick fog blanketed the region that morning, covering the American advance.

D. A thick fog worked as much against as for Washington. His divisions were late or lost.
   1. They had also lost the element of surprise. Hessian Capt. Ewald had been tipped off and passed word on to Howe.
   2. Howe dismissed the information, but the next morning he was awakened by the enemy firing at his headquarters.

E. For a time it seemed both Germantown and the Germantown Pike were open to Washington, but the fog and confusion took a toll.

F. By ten o'clock the Continentals were in retreat and Washington had suffered another defeat.

Suggested Reading:

McGuire, *The Philadelphia Campaign*, chap. 4.

Stephenson, *Patriot Battles*, chap. 17.

Taafe, *The Philadelphia Campaign*, chap. 3.

Questions to Consider:

1. What conclusions can you draw about Washington as a general from his plans at Brandywine and Germantown?

2. What explains Sir William Howe's mysterious decision to move in the opposite direction, away from a junction with Burgoyne?

Lecture Seventeen
With Washington at Valley Forge

Scope: General Howe resigned after hearing about Burgoyne's defeat at Saratoga, and his brother was relieved of his command shortly thereafter. Washington settled the Continental army at Valley Forge for the winter of 1777–1778. The weather was comparatively mild, but the soldiers were ill-clothed and poorly housed, and the food supply systems broke down. The Continental army's soldiers, like the British enlisted men, were mostly from the bottom third of American society and had signed up because they had no better prospects. The officers were much more of a departure from the British norm, as their numbers included more tradesmen than aristocrats. No battle was fought at Valley Forge, except when Washington shrewdly fought off an attempt by Horatio Gates and a faction in Congress to undermine his authority. Another victory for Washington was his appointment of Friedrich von Steuben, a Prussian officer who standardized drill schemes for American regiments. A final triumph occurred when the French ambassador to London announced the signing of new treaties with the Americans.

Outline

I. General Howe had enough men to occupy Philadelphia and keep a watch on Washington but not enough to spare for a major land operation against the river forts the American had constructed on the Delaware River.

    A. On October 23, Sir William and his admiral brother sent five warships to silence Fort Mifflin and prepare the way for an attack by infantry.

        1. The tricky currents of the Delaware caused two British vessels to become grounded.

        2. The burning rafts the Americans sent to destroy one of the stranded vessels instead managed to engulf the 64-gun HMS *Augusta*, which then blew up.

B. Howe's land attack against Fort Mercer went no better.

    1. The commandant of Fort Mercer, Christopher Greene, had cleverly withdrawn his men behind a wall across the interior of the fort.

    2. This turned the north part of the fort into a shooting gallery, and 153 Hessians were killed.

    3. On November 15, the Howe brothers launched another offensive, and this time they battered Fort Mifflin into surrender, which was followed by the evacuation of Fort Mercer.

C. Howe now had an open river supply line to his garrison in Philadelphia—but that was all he had.

D. The news of Burgoyne's surrender at Saratoga horrified Howe.

    1. Not only had he caused the Saratoga debacle by sailing off to Philadelphia, he had also failed to destroy Washington's army.

    2. On October 22, 1777, Howe wrote to Germain offering his resignation, which Germain accepted in February 1778. Admiral "Black Dick" Howe was relieved of his command shortly thereafter.

II. With the onset of winter, Washington and his generals chose to batten down until spring in a site on the west side of the Schuylkill River, 20 miles from Philadelphia, known locally as Valley Forge.

III. The winter of 1777–1778 was difficult for both sides.

A. Sir William Howe had 16,000 British soldiers, Loyalist refugees, prisoners of war, and wives and children of soldiers to feed, adding up to some 37,000 mouths.

B. At the same time, the Continental army did not spend all its time huddled in the snow drifts. The winter of 1777–1778 was comparatively mild, but there were other serious hardships with which to cope.

    1. The plateau on which Washington had laid out his encampment was open, flat, easily defended, and destitute of shelter.

    2. The commissary and quartermaster systems were not functioning, so food came intermittently.

    3. Some of the men were without clothing.

    4. Washington had to organize foraging parties.

    C. Although there was plenty of grumbling among the troops, there was no mutiny.

IV. Who were these men of the new Continental army?

    A. What the muster lists of the Continental regiments is surprising.

        1. As much as 40 percent of the Continentals were foreign-born, and half of that was Irish.

        2. The largest segment was farmers, followed by shoemakers, weavers, and blacksmiths.

        3. The average age was 21 for the American-born, and as high as 29 for the foreign-born. About 14 percent of those foreign-born were convicts sent to the colonies as indentured servants.

        4. Most owned little property.

        5. One must conclude that many of the Continental army's enlistees signed up because they had no better prospects.

    B. The Continental army's officers were largely drawn from the top third of American society, but unlike the top third of British society, many Continental officers followed a trade.

    C. The most dramatic difference between the British and Continental soldier was surely his appearance. Not until 1779 was anything resembling a uniform worn.

    D. For weaponry, the Continentals were armed with the same "Brown Bess" muskets as their British counterparts.

V. There was no "military battle" at Valley Forge, but there were other battles to be fought.

    A. Saratoga had made Horatio Gates a hero as well as a foil for those in the Congress who thought that the main army's problem was Washington.

    B. Gates moved to York, Pennsylvania, and began handing down orders, suggestions, and appointments to Washington.

    C. Washington saw through these schemes and, appealing calmly and skillfully to the president of the Congress, neatly turned the tables on Gates.

    D. He succeeded in getting Nathanael Greene appointed as quartermaster general.

VI. In another great victory at Valley Forge, Washington secured the appointment as his chief of staff Lt. Gen. Baron Friedrich Wilhelm Ludolf Gerhard Augustin von Steuben, late of the personal staff of Frederick the Great, the legendary king of Prussia grew out of his triumph over the so-called "Conway Cabal."

    A. Von Steuben was actually an unemployed half-pay captain in the Prussian army, but his being an ex-Prussian captain was better for Washington because he knew a good deal about drill.

        1. Von Steuben standardized the various drill schemes used in each regiment.

        2. He charmed the Continental soldiers into acquiring a European polish through a combination of multilanguage obscenities and genuine knowledge of his art.

    B. Lafayette and von Steuben were Washington's most valuable foreign assets.

VII. On March 13, the French ambassador in London formally announced his government's new treaties with the Americans. The American war was about to become a world war.

Suggested Reading:

Bodle, *The Valley Forge Winter*, chaps. 5–9.

Fleming, *Washington's Secret War*, chaps. 7–8.

Golway, *Washington's General*, chap. 8.

Questions to Consider:

1. What were the real conditions confronting the Continental army at Valley Forge?

2. What were the contributions made by von Steuben to the survival of the Continental army?

Lecture Eighteen
The Widening War

Scope: The possibility of a French intervention heightened the costs and logistical strain of supplying the British army and the Royal Navy and would require a redeployment of British naval forces. The West Indian planters, with their own voting bloc in Parliament, would oppose any measure that weakened their protections. Parliamentary opposition to the war was growing. Lord Germain accepted Sir William Howe's resignation and ordered the British, under Sir Henry Clinton, to withdraw from Philadelphia to New York. Washington pursued Clinton and caught his rear guard at the Battle of Monmouth Courthouse, in New Jersey, where Charles Lee finally succeeded in completely disgracing himself by retreating. Washington took over Lee's command and successfully led his troops to victory. Washington's war then settled into a stalemate around New York City.

Outline

I. The possibility of a French intervention in the war dramatically heightened the costs and the logistical strain of supplying the British army and navy.

    A. Both might have to confront the French again, if not on the Continent, then certainly in America, the West Indies, Africa, and India.

    B. If Spain followed France, then strategic Gibraltar could be a target.

    C. At worst, the French army might attempt an invasion across the channel.

    D. Even at best, the French navy was a force to be reckoned with.

II. The most likely theater for French trouble-making would be the West Indies.

    A. The British West Indies were staggeringly productive, mainly through the islands' chief product, sugar.

    B. But the West Indian islands were also vulnerable.

        1. Of the half-million settlers in the British West Indies, all but 50,000 were slaves, working under the cruelest of conditions.

    2. This formula ensured rebellion and any threat of war would touch off still more rebellions, especially if the five regiments of military assigned to the islands were called away.

C. There was very little that could be done to reduce this vulnerability, thanks to the lop-sided politics of West Indian sugar. Of the 50,000 whites, the top 1 percent owned 78 percent of the land.

    1. Few of these plantation owners stayed in the West Indies for any length of time; a good percentage sat in Parliament, where they formed the "West India interest."

    2. There would be no defying the West India interest; the question was how much North America would be denuded to defend the islands.

    3. Charles James Fox's motion to send no more reinforcements to America was defeated by only 259 to 165 in the Commons.

    4. The North government authorized a new peace commission to promise the colonies full control over their own internal taxation, no garrisons of regulars in the colonies, recognition of the Continental Congress to speak for the colonies—everything short of independence.

D. Whether this offer placated the Americans or not, the French still had to be dealt with.

    1. In late March 1779, Germain ordered 5,000 of the 16,000 British soldiers in Philadelphia to leave for the West Indies, with another 3,000 to secure the British outposts on the Florida peninsula.

    2. Philadelphia would be abandoned.

    3. The remainder of the British forces in North America would be withdrawn to New York City and Halifax.

E. Sir Henry Clinton, who took over command after Sir William Howe's resignation was accepted, set about preparing to evacuate Philadelphia.

    1. News of the imminent British departure sent into a panic the 4,300 Philadelphians who had taken a loyalty oath to the king.

    2. Some 1,500 Loyalist families took up Clinton's offer to use his transports and left the city.

III. Things seemed to be looking up for Washington.

    A. Conditions at Valley Forge had considerably improved.

        1. Food was regularly available.

2. Von Steuben's drill lessons had whipped the army's brigades into a semblance of European-style uniformity.

3. Enough absentees and recruits had joined the main army that Washington had 15,000 infantry and artillerymen on hand.

B. Benedict Arnold got promoted to major general, and Charles Lee was returned in a prisoner exchange.

C. The North government's peace commission request was turned down with the assurance that the United States had nothing to negotiate.

IV. Not all of this was quite as promising as it seemed.

A. Lafayette, sent on a reconnaissance mission, nearly got cut off and surrounded.

B. Back from captivity, Charles Lee was giving advice again.

1. He began with a reorganization plan for the army.

2. He wrote a letter to Henry Laurens recommending his own promotion to lieutenant general (equal in rank to Washington).

3. He advised Washington not to pursue Clinton into New Jersey, advice Washington did not take.

V. Washington resolutely sprang after Sir Henry Clinton.

A. He left a detachment to occupy Philadelphia and designated Benedict Arnold military commandant of the city.

B. He crossed the rest of the main army over into New Jersey and by June 24 was just north of Princeton and eager to hit Clinton's rear guard.

1. He divided the main army into two corps, the first and lightest under Lee, which caught up with Cornwallis's rear guard near Monmouth Court House (modern Freehold, New Jersey).

2. The other corps, under Washington's direct command, was ready to follow up as soon as Lee made contact.

C. What Lee did not count on was that Cornwallis's rear guard was much bigger than his scouts had led him to believe. Soon Lee's corps was retreating.

D. By noon on June 28, when Washington and the balance of the main army were within 2.5 miles of Monmouth Courthouse, Washington heard no musket fire.

1. Then he began to meet stragglers bearing tales of Lee's retreat, and then Lee and his staff.

2. Washington took command immediately.

E. For the balance of the afternoon, British regulars and Continental line attacked and counterattacked. The temperatures were in the 90s, and men were dying from the heat.
   1. The Americans stood firm, and Washington in particular had handled the situation with skill and confidence.
   2. By morning, the British were gone, and Washington claimed Monmouth as a victory.
F. Formal charges were lodged against Lee, who was found guilty.
G. The British, meanwhile, pushed on to Staten Island.
H. By July 6, Washington had reached the Hudson, north of the British lines around New York City, the same position he had once occupied nearly two years before.

VI. Unbeknownst to Washington, he had fought his last major battle in the north and the next-to-last battle of his entire career. For the next three years, he would settle into conducting the longest—and most unsuccessful—siege in American history around British-held New York.

A. He planted the Continental army in encircling arc of six encampments and began building up forts in the Hudson highlands to secure the Hudson River against any British thrust from the city.

B. Beyond occasional bursts of activity, Washington's war settled into a stalemate around New York City.

Suggested Reading:

Dickinson, ed., *Britain and the American Revolution*, chap. 4.

Shy, *A People Numerous and Armed*, chap. 6.

Taafe, *Philadelphia Campaign*, chap. 6.

Questions to Consider:

1. What impact did the shift of British forces to the protection of the West Indies have on Washington's strategy?

2. In what ways was the Battle at Monmouth Courthouse a moment which justified all of Washington's concepts and actions up until that time?

Lecture Nineteen
The French Menace

Scope: The bulk of the French intervention in the American war for independence would be carried by the French navy. Congress's efforts to create an American navy had been stymied because American ships proved too small to be effective and privateering too lucrative to potential crews. Congress told the navy to recruit its crews from jails or from prisoners of war, so its captains, such as the notorious John Paul Jones, were often taken from the shady side of maritime life. In 1778, the British found that they could protect the channel when Vice-Admiral Augustus Keppel stopped a French fleet from leaving Brest at the Battle of Ushant. However, a fleet from Toulon under the Comte d'Estaing managed to cross the Atlantic to the Delaware Bay and then New York, but twice missed the opportunity to catch Sir Henry Clinton. D'Estaing then sailed to the West Indies, where island to island, the balance of naval power swung back and forth for many months between the British and French fleets.

Outline

I.   France brought to the war a major professional—and newly reorganized—army of nearly 170,000 infantry, 46,000 cavalry, and 12,000 artillerymen.

    A. During the course of this war, this newly reorganized army would fight the British in Ceylon, southern India, the Caribbean, and Florida, and stage raids on the Channel Islands and Canada.

        1. They would not, however, invade the British home islands; the Comte de Vergennes did not want to spread anxiety among the other European kingdoms.

        2. Vergennes committed 27 French battalions to the West Indies.

        3. He would dispatch only nine battalions to help the Americans.

    B. The bulk of the French intervention in the American war for independence would be carried instead by the French navy.

        1. A new naval program was begun after the Seven Years' War.

        2. By the time the American treaties were signed, the new French navy had launched 52 ships of the line; the numbers would reach 73 by 1782.

C. Although the British had superiority in numbers, confidence, and experience, British worries about cross-channel invasion guaranteed that the Royal Navy would be forced to concentrate much of its strength in home water.

D. This left French squadrons free to roam the Atlantic and Caribbean, meeting British squadrons on something close to even terms and providing the Americans with exactly the sort of aid they needed.

    1. The Continental Congress was delighted at the prospect of French gold, weapons, and supplies but was still anxious about having too large a French army presence in North America, lest the French have colonial designs of their own on the American states.

    2. If the principal gift of the French was warships, America would not only gain the navy it lacked, there would be no need for a major French land army in America.

II. Despite the development of a thriving American shipbuilding industry, there was no American naval equivalent of the colonial militia.

A. American shipyards had built only four warships in the century before Lexington and Concord, and none of them distinguished themselves in service or lasted long.

B. As early as September, 1775, Washington commissioned the first Continental navy warships, all converted fishing schooners.

C. Several of the New England states began converting and commissioning vessels of their own, and in October 1775, the Continental Congress authorized the creation of a four-ship American flotilla.

D. A year later, Congress authorized three 74-gun ships of the line, five 36-gun frigates, and an 18-gun two-masted brig.

    1. A successful raid on Nassau emboldened the Continental navy and several of the New England state squadrons to mount a joint attack on a Royal Navy outpost in Penobscot Bay, 110 miles north of Boston, in August of 1776.

    2. But the ships were too small; 14 American ships were lost, and the great ship-building program broke down.

III. It was difficult to generate money or recruits for the navy when privateering was much more lucrative.

    A. Privateering amounted to legalized piracy by allowing private ship owners and their crews to raid enemy merchant shipping and reap the profits.

        1. Such plundering drove British maritime insurance rates up and diverted British naval strength into the business of convoy escort.

        2. Hence, crews and captains, not to mention space in shipyards, were sucked up by privateers who paid far more than the Continental navy.

        3. Congress told the Continental navy to recruit its crews from the common jails or from prisoners of war, and it frequently picked its captains from the dark side of maritime life.

    B. A case in point was John Paul Jones, a Scottish-born merchant officer with a murderous reputation for quarterdeck tyranny.

        1. On September 23, 1779, Jones fought what remains the most famous ship-to-ship action of the war.

        2. Jones was commanding the *Bonhomme Richard* when he challenged the 44-gun British frigate *Serapis* off Flamborough Head.

        3. Jones headed the *Richard* across the *Serapis's* bow and entangled the British frigate's bowsprit in the *Richard's* rigging.

        4. The *Serapis's* captain, Richard Pearson, called on Jones to surrender; Jones defiantly replied, "I haven't yet begun to fight."

        5. Twenty minutes later, a hand grenade tossed from the *Richard* sailed down the *Serapis's* main hatch, set the ready-use ammunition on fire, and forced Capt. Pearson to surrender.

        6. But in the course of the night, the *Richard's* guns had proven defective, and when the crew tried to surrender, Jones turned on them and would have shot them to keep them at their posts.

        7. The *Richard* sank 36 hours after its victory.

    C. Not until nearly the end of the war were the ships of the Continental navy sufficiently well built, crewed, and officered to meet to the British on equal terms in ship-to-ship actions.

IV. What is surprising is not that the Continental navy achieved so little, but that the British navy did not achieve more in the three years before the French intervention.

    A. The Royal Navy expanded after 1775 to between 300 and 400 ships (102 of which carried 50 or more guns) and 110,000 sailors.

    B. But the far reaches of the British Empire were tied to the home islands by the navy, and that meant that when "Black Dick" Howe came out to command the North American station in 1776, he was given only 73 ships and 13,000 sailors to create a blockade, raid coastal towns, and cooperate with the operations of the army.

        1. Howe never had more than seven or eight ships to spare for blockading duties in 1776, and illicit trade between the West Indies and the American rebels was so shameless that the Continental Congress specifically exempted British merchantmen operating out of the Bahamas and Bermuda from capture by American privateers.

        2. Howe was able to increase the number of blockade ships to 20 in 1777, but the energy for blockade waned again in 1778, as Howe had to worry about the French menace.

V. In April 1778, British agents in Paris and Amsterdam learned that a French fleet at Toulon on France's Mediterranean coast was being fitted for sea.

    A. The Toulon fleet, under the command of the Comte d'Estaing, was bound, it was suspected, for the Atlantic and the West Indies.

    B. Another French fleet of ships of the line was still at anchor in Brest, on the Atlantic coast, able to move into the English Channel.

    C. The choices for the Royal Navy were not encouraging.

        1. If the Brest fleet stayed put, the Royal Navy would have to establish some form of blockade, and blockading Brest was not easy.

        2. But neither a "close" blockade nor a "loose" blockade was without severe drawbacks.

    D. The French navy could not ignore the channel, for it was there the British put their primary forces.

        1. Vice-Admiral Augustus Keppel was chosen to command the channel fleet.

        2. When the Brest fleet poked its head into the channel on July 23, 1778, he was ready to meet them with 30 ships of the line.

3. At the Battle of Ushant on July 27, Keppel forced the French to return to their port, thus proving the channel could be kept safe.

E. The Toulon fleet, however, managed to clear the Straits of Gibraltar on May 16, 1778, and headed southwest toward the West Indies.

1. In fact d'Estaing's target was the British North American squadron, and on July 8, 1778, he dropped anchor in the lower Delaware Bay, missing by only three weeks Sir Henry Clinton's crossing of the Delaware.

2. He sailed to intercept the British retreat to New York at Sandy Hook, but he was too late there, too.

3. In August he turned his head toward the West Indies.

VI. The French garrisons in the West Indies had not been idle.

A. On September 7, 1778, a French force of 2,000 landed and seized the island of Dominica with only the faintest resistance.

1. In December 1778, the British struck back and landed on French-held St. Lucia with three brigades of infantry and a flotilla of seven ships under Admiral Samuel Barrington.

2. This was the moment when d'Estaing showed up in the West Indies, but Barrington held firm.

3. D'Estaing carefully veered off again, heading for the friendly French naval base on Martinique.

4. A month later, a British squadron arrived with eight ships of the line to swing the balance of power in the West Indies back again.

B. Admiral d'Estaing recovered a measure of his aggressiveness over the following year, when he successfully orchestrated the seizure of the islands of St. Vincent (in June 1779) and Grenada (in July).

Suggested Reading:

Fowler, *Rebels Under Sail*, chaps. 7, 8, 12.

Miller, *Sea of Glory*, chaps. 5–7, 13–14, 16.

Thomas, *John Paul Jones*, chap. 8–9.

Volo, *Blue Water Patriots*, chaps. 5, 7.

Questions to Consider:

1. Why was privateering more popular than service in the Continental navy?

2. What was France's principal contribution to the American war effort, and why was this so important?

Lecture Twenty
Vain Hopes in the Carolinas

Scope: Sir Henry Clinton's success on various small campaigns in the South, including the capture of Savannah, led him and Lord Germain to think that perhaps British victory might be found by turning attention southward. This idea was no doubt reinforced after the new Commander of the Continental army's Southern Department, Maj. Gen. Benjamin Lincoln, mounted an unsuccessful effort to recapture Savannah and shortly thereafter, was forced to accept Clinton's demand of an unconditional surrender during the British siege of Charleston. Clinton's army began occupying the strategic posts in the area and adding Loyalist volunteers to their number, allowing a confident Clinton to depart and leave the occupation of the Carolinas to Charles Earl Cornwallis. Clinton and Germain found, however, that they could not always depend on the Loyalists, and the British defeats at the Battles of Cowpens and King's Mountain further jeopardized British hopes for victory.

Outline

I. Despite his feeling of self-pity at being handed command of an army whose strength had been stripped by half, Sir Henry Clinton responded decisively to Lord Germain's directive to bring Mr. Washington to action.

   A. He ordered the burning of Portsmouth and Norfolk in the Chesapeake and commanded a destructive raid along the Long Island Sound.

   B. In another successful raid, a British regiment and two battalions of Hessians overran Savannah's feeble defenses and struck inland to Augusta.

   C. A Swiss-born British officer named Prevost then made his way to the gates of Charleston.

   D. Germain was delighted at the news of the capture of Savannah and the occupation of Georgia: Perhaps victory just might be snatched from the jaws of defeat in America by turning attention southward.

II. Maj. Gen. Benjamin Lincoln arrived to take command of the Continental army's Southern Department in January of 1779.

    A. In tandem with the French fleet from the West Indies, he tried unsuccessfully to mount an attack on Savannah, resulting in 521 wounded and 223 dead.

    B. Lincoln's failure to retake Savannah convinced Sir Henry Clinton that the southern colonies were ripe for a major picking.

        1. In late 1779 Clinton assembled a navy fleet of more than 100 vessels as well as a large, experienced expeditionary and embarked them on December 19.

        2. Bad weather kept them at sea until February 1, when they were finally able to drop anchor in the Savannah River.

        3. By mid-February, lookouts in Charleston could spot the campfires of Clinton's army.

III. Meanwhile Lincoln and Washington had prepared for the British to take a second swipe at Charleston, and the citizens of the city were confident that they would be able to defend their city again.

    A. But by March 20, however, the British threatened Charleston from land and sea.

    B. The siege was not easy, but Continentals were proved outmatched.

        1. On April 13, Lincoln's principal officers urged a breakout attempt.

        2. The next day Tarleton's dragoons defeated Lincoln's cavalry at Monck's Corner.

        3. On May 6, Ft. Moultrie was captured by British seamen and marines.

        4. On May 8, Lincoln asked Sir Henry Clinton for terms of surrender for the entire garrison.

        5. May 11, Lincoln gave in to Clinton's terms of unconditional surrender.

IV. The fall of Charleston was a low point for the Americans.

    A. Clinton's army began occupying the strategic posts in the area and adding Loyalist volunteers to their number.

    B. In late May, Tarleton's dragoons massacred Abraham Buford's 3rd regiment of Virginia Continentals.

    C. In June, Clinton returned to New York City and left the occupation of the Carolinas in to Charles Earl Cornwallis.

V. To add insult to injury, Lincoln's replacement was Horatio Gates, who immediately decided to go on campaign.

    A. Gates hoped to be able to make a defensive stand near Camden, South Carolina, and he got exactly what he wanted.

    B. The cavalry detachments of the two armies collided near Camden on August 15. Gates's determination to fight only a defensive battle proved disastrous as Cornwallis's regulars attacked.

        1. The North Carolina militia saw oncoming British bayonets and fled in panic.

        2. Cornwallis's regulars and Tarleton's dragoons smashed into the Maryland and Delaware Continentals.

        3. Gates turned and rode for his life, stopping only at Hillsborough, North Carolina, 180 miles away.

        4. Less then two months later, Horatio Gates was relieved of command of the Southern Department.

VI. Clinton and Germain had exaggerated the dependence they thought they could place on the Loyalists, for they found that people swore allegiance to the Crown one day, only to swear allegiance to the Continental Congress the next.

    A. In the Camden district, rebel militiamen took an oath to the king and as soon as they were issued weapons, deserted and rejoined the rebels.

    B. British officers recruited Loyalists to man their advanced outposts, only to find that the Loyalist militia deserted as soon as the officers moved on.

VII. Rival militias soon substituted long-time revenge for any real identification with rebels or king's men.

    A. In October 1780 at King's Mountain near Charlotte, more than 1,000 Loyalists frantically fought rebel militia, leaving 300 dead or wounded and 700 taken prisoner.

    B. Banastre Tarleton and his dragoons in particular were a target for rebel vengeance.

        1. Daniel Morgan tricked Tarleton into a cleverly planned trap at the Battle of Cowpens, where more than 100 British and Loyalists were killed, another 200 wounded, and 527 captured.

        2. Tarleton barely escaped, only to have to report his disaster to Cornwallis.

C. Neither the Battle of Cowpens nor King's Mountain was a large-scale battle, but together, they spelled doom for Sir Henry Clinton's hopes for British victory.

Suggested Reading:

Babits, *A Devil of a Whipping*, chaps. 4–8.

Borick, *A Gallant Defense*, chaps. 7–13.

Buchanan, *Road to Guildford Courthouse*, chaps. 4–5, 12.

Questions to Consider:

1. How effective a field commander was Sir Henry Clinton compared to his predecessor, Sir William Howe?

2. What was Horatio Gates's key tactical mistake at Camden?

Lecture Twenty-One
"The Americans Fought Like Demons"

Scope: After serving Washington successfully as quartermaster, Nathanael Greene was appointed to take over the Southern army after Horatio Gates's defeat at Camden. Greene determined that his Continental troops had plenty of ways to combat the British apart from open battle, including encouraging the backcountry warfare waged by Francis Marion and other rebel militia and setting up a series of boat caches to cross the ladder of rivers that crossed the Carolina coastal plain. It was at the Battle of Guildford Courthouse, though, where Greene forced Cornwallis to admit that the Americans could in fact "fight like demons."

Outline

I. Nathanael Greene, Washington's most successful quartermaster general, was just the person to pull the disaster-wracked Southern Department of the Continental army into order.

   A. He was born in 1742 into a family of Quakers, but he had an aggressive spirit that bent him toward books and that led to his suspension from the family's Quaker meeting in 1773. He never looked back.

      1. As commander of the Rhode Island militia, he met George Washington for the first time on July 4, 1775, in the Continental army's first encampment outside Boston.

      2. Washington prevailed on the Continental Congress to commission Nathanael Greene as a brigadier general in the Continental army.

   B. Although Greene's development as an officer required patience on Washington's part, in February of 1778, Washington proposed making Nathanael Greene quartermaster general of the main army.

      1. Greene wanted very badly to refuse, but he succeeded admirably at the job.

      2. Greene reorganized purchasing, created an army script known as "quartermaster's certificates," and set up magazines and storage depots at strategic points along the army's routes of campaign.

II. After the disaster at Camden, Washington moved Greene into Gates's place, for Greene had a practical eye for what armies could and could not do.

    A. First, the Southern army could not rebuild itself far enough or fast enough to confront Earl Cornwallis' army in an open fight.

    B. Second, the vicious partisan warfare being waged throughout the backcountry made it impossible for the British to supply themselves successfully from the countryside or to provide reinforcements and replacements for their casualties and losses.

    C. It thus became Nathanael Greene's business to keep his army away from any match with Cornwallis, while allowing Francis Marion and the partisans to undermine British control of the countryside.

    D. Greene brought with him a detachment of cavalry under "Light-horse Harry" Lee to supplement William Washington's dragoons, so that Greene would always have greater mounted scouting resources than Cornwallis.

    E. Greene convinced Francis Marion to provide intelligence-gathering and to identify supply sources.

    F. Above all, Greene wanted caches of boats to allow his troops to cross safely and easily the ladder of parallel rivers, all the way up into Virginia to the James River.

III. Greene would not sit idle.

    A. He detached Daniel Morgan and the Maryland and Delaware Continentals, who defeated Banastre Tarleton at Cowpens, a small but costly battle for the British on January 17, 1781.

    B. In January and February 1781, Greene lured Cornwallis across the Carolina Piedmont, where Greene's caches of boats came to his troops rescue, first at the Yadkin River and then at the Dan River, just over the line in Virginia.

IV. From the perspective of Lord George Germain in London, little stood between Cornwallis and a triumphant link with the British occupation forces in Portsmouth and Norfolk.

    A. Germain did not know that Cornwallis was 150 miles from the nearest usable supply station at Wilmington, North Carolina, nor that there was no British garrison in Portsmouth or Norfolk.

    B. And any hope that North Carolina Loyalists would turn out to help Cornwallis vanished on February 25, when "Light-Horse Harry"

Lee fooled 400 Loyalists into thinking that the Americans were Tarleton's dragoons, and then cut them to pieces.

    C. Cornwallis had no choice but to stop his pursuit of Greene.

V. Now it was Greene's turn to chase Cornwallis.

    A. Reinforced by two brigades of North Carolina militia, Greene slipped eastward to Guildford Courthouse, near modern Greensboro, North Carolina, on March 14. There the Earl decided to turn and grapple with his tormentor.

    B. For once, Greene would risk an open fight, but he would do it on the defensive, imitating Morgan's tactical plan at Cowpens.

    C. It was not quite the climactic event that either man had been waiting for.

        1. A series of volleys, advances, and pullbacks on both sides resulted at one point in such a logjam that Cornwallis ordered his artillery to fire into the struggling mass of men, killing friend and enemy alike.

        2. On March 15, 1781, Greene called for a general retreat, not wanting to lose more of his Continentals.

        3. Cornwallis wanted to pursue but his men were too winded, and too many had been killed or were wounded. Rain fell that night, adding to the misery for the British.

    D. Cornwallis issued a proclamation, claiming victory, but he later admitted that the Americans had fought admirably.

Suggested Reading:

Buchanan, *Road to Guildford Courthouse*, chaps. 23–24.

Pancake, *This Destructive War*, chaps. 6–8, 11.

Stephenson, *Patriot Battles*, chap. 21.

Questions to Consider:

1. How did Nathanael Greene's experience in providing for supply and logistics for the Continental army help him in planning strategy in the Carolinas?

2. Why were the British unable to sustain their initial successes in the Carolinas?

Lecture Twenty-Two
The Reward of Loyalty

Scope: Those who remained loyal to Britain did not have an easy time during the revolution. Some families had been torn apart by contrary allegiances. Some became the subject of rebel rampage and suffered loss of property and even loss of life. The biggest losers however, were the Indians, many of whom had established centuries-long ties with the British. The Iroquois, Cherokee, and Shawnee all fought bitter battles with militia and suffered destruction and loss of their native land. Washington saw rebellion closer to home in the form of the Pennsylvania Continentals, who mutinied in January 1781. Far more painful for Washington, however, was the shocking mutiny of Benedict Arnold.

Outline

I. In January 1781, Washington feared that American society might be incapable of sustaining the war effort.

    A. Sometimes contrary allegiances tore families in half.

    B. Loyalists became the targets of rebel rage and even legislation.

        1. The New York legislature made it a felony to promote Loyalism and the estates of prominent Loyalists were confiscated and broken up.

        2. In North Carolina, Loyalists were given 60 days to sell their property and leave, or else face confiscation.

        3. In Georgia, the rebel legislature declared 117 persons guilty of treason and confiscated their possessions.

II. The biggest losers for Loyalism, however, were the 200,000 Indians who had been driven into a narrowing band of territory between the Appalachian foothills and the Mississippi River.

    A. The Iroquois Nations of upstate New York were reluctant to commit themselves to one or the other side

        1. In 1777 Joseph Brant, a Mohawk himself, was successful in bringing four of the six Iroquois tribes over to the British side.

        2. Starting in the summer of 1778, a combined force of Loyalists and British Iroquois swept down the Susquehanna River, destroying a militia outpost and massacring hundreds.

3. This massacre brought on a series of retaliation on both sides, which finally led Washington to order an entire division of Continentals led by John Sullivan to eliminate the Iroquois threat on the northern frontier.

4. The clash of the Sullivan expedition with the Loyalist-Iroquois allies at present-day Elmira was just the start of a series of mutual retaliations resulting in the ravage of the entire region of the old Iroquois confederacy in upstate New York and upper Pennsylvania.

B. Much the same pattern repeated itself further to the south, where the Shawnee and the Cherokee had long stood in the path of colonial expansion.

1. In March 1775, to the dismay of a number of Cherokee, a land development company persuaded the Cherokee leadership to sell 27,000 square miles (the equivalent of the modern state of Kentucky) to the Transylvania Company for approximately £10,000 in trade goods.

2. In July 1776, a Cherokee leader, Dragging Canoe, forced settlers to withdraw into three fortified towns, but the Cherokee were, in turn, attacked by South Carolina and North Carolina militia.

C. The next year, the Shawnee attacked Harrodsburg in March and besieged Boonesborough from April to May 1777, and capturing Daniel Boone himself in February 1778.

1. In reply, Virginia governor Patrick Henry authorized Lt. Col. George Rogers Clark and the Virginia militia to conduct a counteroffensive, not against the Shawnee or the Cherokee, but across the Ohio River, at the real source of the Indian troubles, the British outposts at Kaskaskia and Vincennes (in modern-day Illinois and Indiana).

2. Clark surprised and overran the tiny garrison at Kaskaskia on July 4, 1778, without firing a single shot.

3. On February 5, 1779, Clark marched out of Kaskaskia with 200 men and on February 24, delivered a summons to Lt. Gov. Hamilton to surrender, to which Hamilton eventually agreed.

D. In later years, the Indians, both Shawnee and Cherokee, suffered greatly.

1. Most of the Cherokee sued for peace in 1777 and signed the first United States Indian treaty in 1785; by 1800, the

Cherokee had withdrawn into northern Georgia and were then deported in 1834, along the tragic "Trail of Tears," to modern-day Oklahoma.

2. The Shawnee fought on until 1794, when "Mad Anthony" Wayne defeated them at Fallen Timbers. A new generation of Shawnee was defeated by an American army at Tippecanoe in 1811 and the Battle of the Thames in 1813.

III. Washington was also plagued by mutiny and disloyalty within the army.

A. The army went unpaid, unfed, and unclothed.

1. On New Year's Day, 1781, the Pennsylvania Continentals seized the brigade artillery and formed up to march away to Philadelphia.

2. A compromise was hammered out guaranteeing new clothing and pay warrants.

B. But for Washington, the most painful incident of mutiny concerned the unhappy Benedict Arnold.

1. Washington had tried to mollify Arnold by securing him a promotion to major general and assigning him as commandant of a reoccupied Philadelphia in 1778.

2. Through his young Loyalist wife Peggy, Arnold began furtively corresponding with Sir Henry Clinton's adjutant-general, Maj. John André.

3. In the summer of 1780, Washington appointed Arnold commandant of West Point.

4. In July, Arnold got an offer of £20,000 and a general's commission in the British army for the betrayal of West Point and, if possible, George Washington.

5. In September 1780, André was stopped as he tried to make his way through American lines in disguise; the plans and schedule Arnold had given him for capturing West Point were found.

6. Arnold soon learned he had been discovered and made his way safely to New York. André was hanged.

7. Washington arrived at West Point on September 25 and was stunned to discover Arnold missing and the envelope of incriminating papers.

Suggested Reading:

Hammon & Taylor, *Virginia's Western War*, chap. 4.

Nash, *The Unknown American Revolution*, chap. 7.

Randall, *Benedict Arnold*, chaps. 17–19.

Walsh, *The Execution of Major André*, chaps. 5–7.

Questions to Consider:

1. Why didn't the British take advantage of the mutiny of the Pennsylvania Continentals?

2. Should Sir Henry Clinton have agreed to exchange Arnold for André?

Lecture Twenty-Three
A Sword for General Washington

Scope: Cornwallis's tactical plans had worked for almost two years, but eventually, he determined to move into Virginia to cut off wily Nathanael Greene's supply and recruiting sources and to establish a naval station. Washington's army meanwhile had thought the war would end in New York City, but the general's desire to capture Benedict Arnold and the arrival of French troops and ships caused him to rethink his tactics and move his army southward. After Cornwallis had managed to establish Yorktown as a supply and naval station, the British commander's grand plans began to fall apart. He underestimated American and French strength, and help from the British navy and Clinton's promise for troop reinforcements proved too little too late. On October 17, 1781, he ordered a flag of truce be presented. The official surrender documents were signed on October 19.

Outline

I. Charles Cornwallis's plan for keeping British hopes in North America alive involved four parts:

    A. Hold New York City.

    B. Stage raids along the vulnerable American coastline.

    C. Pacify the Georgia and South Carolina interior with a network of small fortified Loyalist garrisons.

    D. Reserve Cornwallis's small British field army for mopping up the feeble Continental resistance left in the South.

II. For almost two years, this plan had worked, but Nathanael Greene proved an elusive and clever opponent.

    A. By April of 1781, Cornwallis determined to strike northward into Virginia, where Greene's supply and recruiting grounds lay.

    B. Cornwallis was encouraged to move into Virginia by two other events.

        1. Lord Francis Rawdon had beaten off Greene's Continentals at Hobkirk's Hill on April 25, so the South Carolina garrisons looked capable of keeping the peace there if Cornwallis wanted to move northward.

2. A British raiding expedition commanded by Benedict Arnold had descended on Virginia almost without opposition, up the James River.

3. He marched out of Wilmington with Banastre Tarleton, a few dragoons, and about 1,435 men.

III. For two years, George Washington's main army was convinced that the war would be ended only when Sir Henry Clinton either left New York and gave battle or else ran too low on hope or supplies.

   A. Even when the French finally began shipping troops to North America in April 1780 under the command of the Viscomte de Rochambeau, they showed no eagerness to join in any assault on New York.

   B. However, more than New York City, Washington wanted Benedict Arnold. A three-battalion force led by the Marquis de Lafayette tried unsuccessfully to chase down Arnold.

   C. Cornwallis's main aim was Portsmouth, but when he saw the difficult terrain around Portsmouth, he chose Yorktown.

IV. At this point Cornwallis's plans began to unravel.

   A. Important British commanders, including Arnold, took ill. Greene and his Continental troops continued to foil British plans.

   B. By the summer 1781, all that was left of the British conquests of 1780 was the coastal strip between Charleston and Savannah.

   C. The bloody Battle at Eutaw Springs, on September 8, proved to be the British army's last fight in South Carolina.

V. The ultimate blow to Cornwallis's strategy was the one he dealt himself.

   A. Washington could not let Lafayette stay within reach of Cornwallis's army in Virginia and so determined to turn his views southward.

      1. News came that Admiral François-Joseph-Paul, the Comte de Grasse, and a French fleet would make a pass at the North American mainland in the fall.

      2. Washington faced southward with the bulk of the Continentals on August 21, followed shortly by Rochambeau and the French.

   B. Cornwallis had little reason to worry about warnings of Washington's movements.

      1. He continued to launch search-and-destroy missions into Virginia and began constructing entrenchments to protect Yorktown.

    2. However, Admiral Sir George Rodney, commander of the British West Indies squadron, made a series of tactical mistakes that enabled the French fleet to enter the Chesapeake without incident.

  C. When the French ships arrived, Cornwallis realized he could leave Yorktown and elude both Lafayette to the south and Washington and Rochambeau to the north.

    1. Thanks to Admiral Hood's appearance off the Virginia capes and a message from Sir Henry Clinton promising reinforcements, Cornwallis chose to stay.

    2. The truth was that Clinton could send no reinforcements before mid-October, and by September 26, Washington had pinned Cornwallis against the York River.

VI. Cornwallis's army was greatly outnumbered, outarmed, and outmaneuvered.

  A. He had only one other general officer to assist him, Charles O'Hara, while Washington had Knox, Lafayette, Baron von Steuben, and Benjamin Lincoln.

  B. On October 9, American and French artillery began raining shot down on the heads of the British garrison, on the buildings in Yorktown, on the waterfront, and on the British ships.

  C. Meanwhile, American and French troops dug trenches toward the British lines and on October 14 stormed the redoubts.

  D. On October 16, Cornwallis decided to abandon Yorktown but a violent storm dashed his plans. The next day, he ordered a flag of truce to be presented.

  E. The official surrender documents were signed on October 19.

Suggested Reading:

Johnston, *The Yorktown Campaign*, chaps. 6–7.

Ketchum, *Victory at Yorktown*, chaps. 8–9.

Selby, *The Revolution in Virginia*, chaps. 14–15.

Questions to Consider:

1. What role did the French play in the American victory at Yorktown?

2. Who was most at fault for the loss of Yorktown within the British leadership?

Lecture Twenty-Four
"It Is All Over"

Scope: After Cornwallis's defeat at Yorktown, it seemed that only King George III believed the war was worth continuing. A motion to end the war was finally passed in Parliament in February 1782, and shortly thereafter, Lord North's entire cabinet resigned. To the dismay of the French, an American team consisting of John Jay, Samuel Adams, Benjamin Franklin, and Henry Laurens negotiated a unilateral treaty with Britain. At war's end, many on the "losing side," including John Peebles, Johann Ewald, and even Benedict Arnold, went on to distinguished and successful careers. The bigger losers were the Loyalists and the black slaves who joined the British in pursuit of freedom. Both the winning and losing sides were astonished when the indispensable George Washington returned to civilian life, as did many of the soldiers who served under him, including Horatio Gates, Nathanael Greene, and Daniel Morgan. For most Americans, though, the significance of this war was that it had established among them a consciousness that this is "my country."

Outline

I. In Britain, the news of a second loss to the Americans made the war look hopeless.

    A. Perhaps the only man who still believed that the war was worth continuing was King George III.

        1. The king remained confident that his army would carry on after the shock of the bad news wore off.

        2. The government, however, had been losing ground to Charles James Fox and the Whig opposition.

        3. Spain entered the war on the side of France and the Americans and was later joined by the Dutch, who had been annoying the British government all through the war.

    B. On December 4, 1781, Edmund Burke started the opposition landslide in Parliament.

        1. On February 28, 1782, a renewed motion to end the war passed by 19 votes.

    2. Germain resigned and Lord North announced the resignation of the entire cabinet, including himself.

    3. North was replaced by a Whig the king detested, the elderly Charles Watson-Wentworth, the 2nd Marquess of Rockingham and the new Secretaries of State would be Shelburne and Fox.

II. The suspension of the fighting in America was not, however, the end of the war.

    A. The French recaptured St. Eustatia in November 1781.

    B. In April of 1782, de Grasse's expedition to conquer Jamaica failed.

    C. In India, the French tried unsuccessfully to rouse a coalition of Indian princes against the British East India Company.

III. The new Rockingham administration did not rush toward a final peace.

    A. Shelburne hoped for some arrangement short of outright independence.

    B. Benjamin Franklin proposed that the Americans might be willing to make a separate peace if Britain ceded Canada to American control.

    C. Franklin, Henry Laurens, John Jay, and John Adams formed the American negotiating team.

    D. Jay pushed for a unilateral peace treaty with Britain, warning Franklin that it was not in the best interest of France to have a strong and independent United States.

    E. In mid-October 1782, a preliminary agreement was reached in talks between the Americans and Shelburne, who become prime minister when Rockingham died.

        1. It conceded American Independence.

        2. It fixed the western boundary of the United States at the Mississippi River.

        3. It set a boundary between British Canada and the United States along the Great Lakes and below the St. Lawrence River.

    F. On December 5, King George III opened yet another Parliament and from the throne declared America "… free and independent States. …" The final treaty was signed on September 3, 1783.

IV. There were losers in the American Revolution, although some of the losers did not do badly.

    A. Capt. John Peebles of the 42nd Regiment (the Black Watch) sold out his commission in the 42nd and went home in 1782.

    B. Capt. Johann Ewald was paroled back to the British garrison in New York and soon after signed up for service under the king of Denmark, under whom he made major general.

    C. Sir William Howe lost his seat in Parliament in 1780, but the king appointed him lieutenant general of ordnance in 1782.

    D. Banastre Tarleton went up the ladder of army promotion and found a second career representing Liverpool in Parliament.

    E. Charles, Earl Cornwallis, was appointed governor-general of India in 1786 and remains one of the key figures in the creation of British India.

    F. Lord George Germain retired to his estates in Sussex.

    G. Benedict Arnold set himself up in the West India trade.

V. The big losers were the Loyalists.

    A. Fifteen thousand Loyalist refugees flooded into Nova Scotia, becoming the new governing elite of Canada.

    B. The black slaves who had joined the British in pursuit of their freedom were far bigger losers.

        1. Over the course of the war, upward of 80,000 American slaves ran away, joined the British, or found some way to freedom. After the Paris Treaty was signed, the British denied any responsibility for them.

        2. Some were shipped to Nova Scotia; some formed the core of a black colony on the west coast of Africa, Sierra Leone. Others were sold back into slavery.

VI. After the preliminary treaty in November 1782, the Continental Congress began planning the demobilization of its army, irrespective of whether its soldiers had been paid the money Congress owed them or its officers granted the pensions George Washington had demanded for them.

    A. Washington had to be vigilant for both the British who still sullenly occupied New York and for the whiffs of mutiny from his own ranks.

B. In March 1783, Washington addressed some of his officers to quash a rumored conspiracy to march on Philadelphia and install him as king.

VII. By 1783, everyone on both sides of the war knew that George Washington had been America's indispensable man.

    A. He had lost more battles than he had won, but time and again he had saved his army to fight again.

    B. He had proven resourceful and flexible, dignified without arrogance.

    C. With the peace terms settled, he led the army back into New York City as the British pulled out. He later announced his intention to resign and return to civilian life.

VIII. The soldiers Washington had led also faded back into private lives once Congress officially disbanded the army in June 1784.

    A. Horatio Gates left the army in 1784 and moved to New York City. He even served a term in the New York legislature.

    B. Henry Knox succeeded Washington in command of the army and then followed Washington in politics as secretary of war when Washington was elected president of the United States.

    C. Nathanael Greene used the bounties and lands voted him by Congress for his service to pay the outstanding bills of his Southern army.

    D. Charles Lee did not live to see the peace treaty signed, dying in Philadelphia in 1782.

    E. Daniel Morgan amassed a fortune in real estate in the Shenandoah Valley.

    F. "Mad Anthony" Wayne was elected to a seat in the Pennsylvania state legislature; he then moved to Georgia, where he was elected to Congress, and then took command of the American army.

IX. American soldiers had fought in 1,200 battles, skirmishes, and sieges, and lost over 10,000 killed and wounded.

    A. These soldiers not only secured American Independence, they developed a sense of common nationality.

    B. It would take another 80 years of political strife to finish the beginnings of this work, but it would be the foundation of "an empire for liberty."

Suggested Reading:

Morris, *The Peacemakers*, chaps. 15–16.

Norton, *The British Americans*, chaps. 7–8.

Weintraub, *Iron Tears*, chap. 14–15.

Questions to Consider:

1. Was the king's hope of continuing the war a delusion?
2. Why was Washington's resignation as commander of the army so remarkable?

Maps and Battle Plans
The Thirteen Colonies

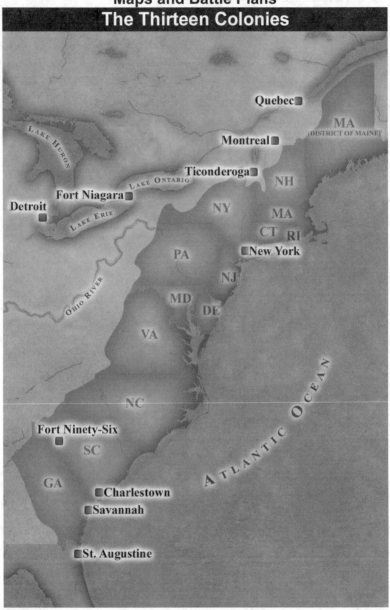

Quebec

MA
(DISTRICT OF MAINE)

Montreal

Ticonderoga

NH

LAKE HURON

Fort Niagara

LAKE ONTARIO

NY

MA

Detroit

LAKE ERIE

CT RI

New York

PA

NJ

OHIO RIVER

MD

DE

VA

NC

ATLANTIC OCEAN

Fort Ninety-Six

SC

GA

Charlestown

Savannah

St. Augustine

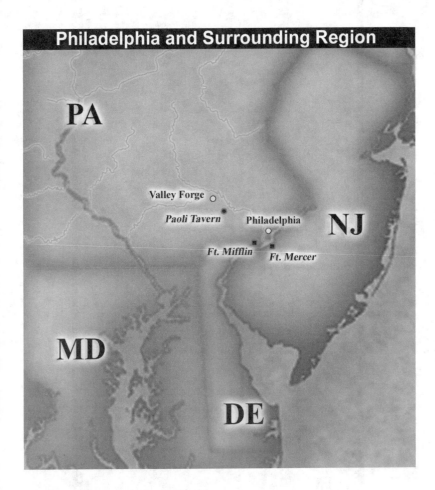

Philadelphia and Surrounding Region

PA

NJ

MD

DE

Valley Forge

Paoli Tavern

Philadelphia

Ft. Mifflin

Ft. Mercer

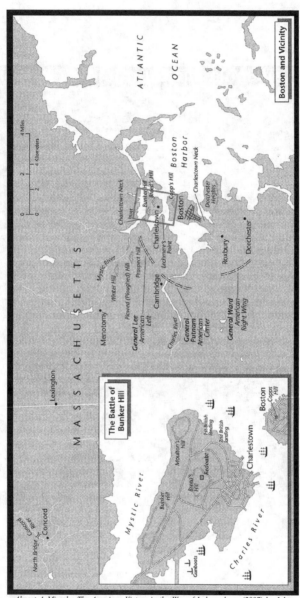

Almost A Miracle: The American Victory in the War of Independence (2007) by John Ferling. By **permission of Oxford University Press, Inc.**

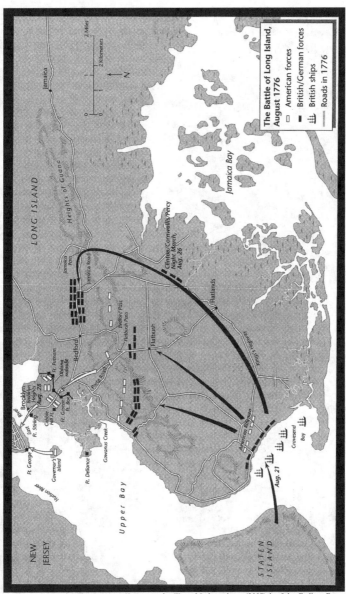

Almost A Miracle: The American Victory in the War of Independence (2007) by John Ferling. By **permission of Oxford University Press, Inc.**

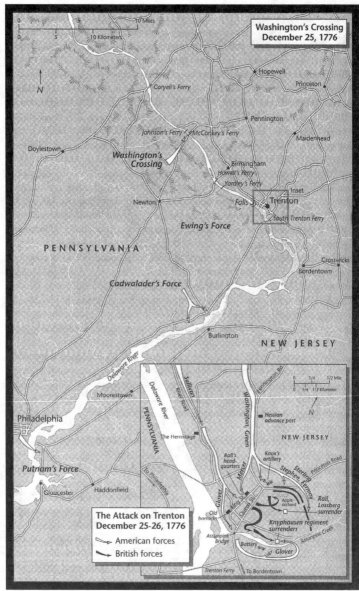

Almost A Miracle: The American Victory in the War of Independence (2007) by John Ferling. By **permission of Oxford University Press, Inc.**

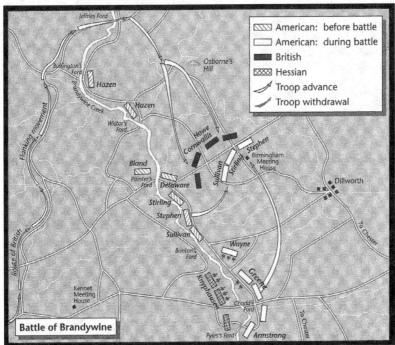

Almost A Miracle: The American Victory in the War of Independence (2007) by John Ferling. By **permission of Oxford University Press, Inc.**

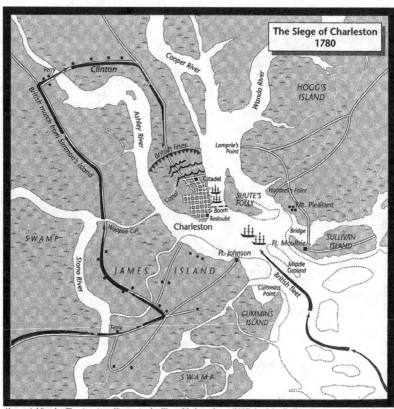

The Siege of Charleston
1780

Cooper River

Clinton

Ferry

British march from Simmon's Island

Ashley River

HOGG'S ISLAND

Wando River

British lines

Lamprie's Point

Citadel

SHUTE'S FOLLY

Haddrell's Point

Mt. Pleasant

Canal

Boom

Redoubt

Charleston

Wappoo Cut

SWAMP

Stono River

JAMES   ISLAND

Ft. Johnson

Ft. Moultrie

Bridge

SULLIVAN ISLAND

Middle Ground

British fleet

Ferry

Cummins Point

CUMMINS ISLAND

SWAMP

Almost A Miracle: The American Victory in the War of Independence (2007) by John Ferling. By **permission of Oxford University Press, Inc.**

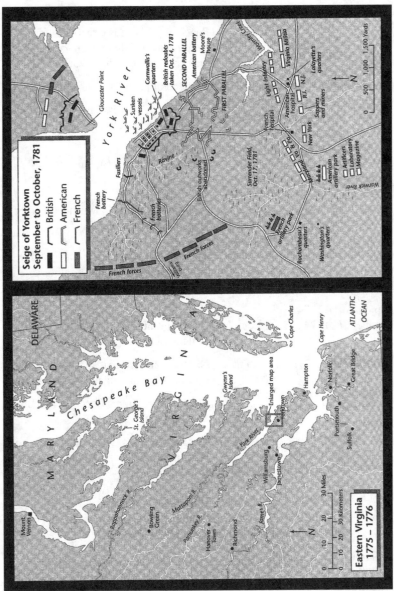

Almost A Miracle: The American Victory in the War of Independence (2007) by John Ferling. By **permission of Oxford University Press, Inc.**

Timeline

February 10, 1763 .... Peace of Paris ends Great War for Empire (also called Seven Years' War and French and Indian War).

March 22, 1765 .... Parliament passes Stamp Act.

October 19, 1765 .... Stamp Act Congress ratifies John Dickinson's "Declaration of Rights and Grievances."

March 18, 1766 .... Parliament repeals Stamp Act.

March 5, 1770 .... Boston Massacre.

April 12, 1770 .... Parliament repeals Townshend Duties, except for tax on tea.

December 16, 1773 .... Boston Tea Party.

March 31–June 22, 1774 .... Parliament retaliates with Intolerable Acts.

September 5, 1774–
October 26, 1774 .... First Continental Congress meets in Philadelphia.

April 18–19, 1775 .... Clashes between British troops and militia at Lexington and Concord.

May 10, 1775 .... Ethan Allen and his Green Mountain Boys seize Ticonderoga.

June 14–15, 1775 .... Congress creates Continental army and commissions Washington as its commander.

June 17, 1775 .... Battle of Bunker Hill.

August 23, 1775 .... George III declares colonies in a state of rebellion.

September–December 1775 .... Montgomery and Arnold's campaign into Canada.

October 10, 1775.............................Howe succeeds Gage as British commander in chief in America.

November 10, 1775..........................Formation of U.S. Marine Corps.

November 28, 1775..........................Formation of U.S. Navy.

January 10, 1776.............................Publication of Tom Paine's *Common Sense.*

March 17, 1776...............................British evacuate Boston.

June 7, 1776....................................Richard Henry Lee moves for independence in Continental Congress.

June 28, 1776..................................British fail to take Charleston.

July 4, 1776....................................Congress endorses Jefferson's Declaration of Independence.

July 12, 1776..................................Congress begins debate on Articles of Confederation.

August 27, 1776..............................Washington defeated at Long Island.

August 30, 1777..............................Washington evacuates Long Island under cover of darkness.

September 15, 1776..........................Howe lands at Kip's Bay and seizes control of lower Manhattan.

September 22, 1776..........................Nathan Hale hung by the British as a spy.

October 11, 1776.............................Carleton defeats Arnold at Valcour Island.

October 28, 1776.............................Battle of White Plains.

November 15–16, 1776....................Fall of Fort Lee.

November 19–20, 1776....................Fall of Fort Washington.

December 26, 1776..........................Washington defeats British and Hessians at Trenton.

January 3, 1777...............................Washington defeats British at Princeton.

June 14, 1777..................................Adoption of the Stars and Stripes.

July 6, 1777	Burgoyne captures Ticonderoga.
September 11, 1777	Washington defeated at Brandywine.
October 4, 1777	Washington defeated at Germantown.
October 17, 1777	Burgoyne surrenders to Gates at Saratoga.
October 22, 1777	Hessian attack on Fort Mercer fails to open Delaware River.
December 18, 1777	Washington marches into encampment at Valley Forge.
February 6, 1778	Treaty of Amity and Commerce signed with France.
May 8, 1778	Howe replaced by Clinton.
June 18, 1778	Clinton evacuates Philadelphia.
June 28, 1778	Battle of Monmouth Courthouse.
July 3, 1778	Wyoming Valley Massacre.
July 4, 1778	George Rogers Clark seizes Kaskaskia.
July 27, 1778	Battle of Ushant.
November 11, 1778	Cherry Valley Massacre.
December 29, 1778	British capture Savannah.
February 25, 1779	George Rogers Clark captures Vincennes.
April 12, 1779	Spain joins war.
June 16, 1779	French fleet captures St. Vincent.
June 21, 1779	Spanish begin siege of Gibraltar.
July 15, 1779	Americans capture Stony Point.
August 19, 1779	Americans capture Paulus Hook.
August 29, 1779	Sullivan defeats combined Loyalist-Iroquois force at Newtown.
September 23, 1779	John Paul Jones defeats *Serapis*.

October 11, 1779.............................. Clinton evacuates Rhode Island.

January 16–17, 1780 .... Battle of Cape St. Vincent.

May 12, 1780 .... Charleston falls to Clinton.

July 11, 1780................................. Rochambeau's army arrives at Newport.

August 15–16, 1780........................ Gates defeated at battle of Camden.

September 25, 1780 .... Benedict Arnold flees to safety with British, abandoning John André to be hung as a spy on October 2.

October 7, 1780.............................. Rebel militia victorious over Patrick Ferguson at King's Mountain.

January 1, 1781 .... Mutiny of the Pennsylvania Continentals.

January 17, 1781 .... Daniel Morgan defeats Tarleton at battle of Cowpens.

March 15, 1781 .... Cornwallis wins Pyrrhic victory at Guildford Courthouse.

September 8, 1781 .... Greene defeated at Eutaw Springs.

September 30–
October 19, 1781............................ Cornwallis forced into siege at Yorktown and surrenders.

February 28, 1782 .... Parliament votes to discontinue military operations in America.

July 1, 1782................................... Death of the Earl of Rockingham; succeeded by Lord Shelburne.

April 4, 1782.................................. Clinton replaced by Sir Guy Carleton as commander in chief in America.

April 12, 1782................................ Battle of the Saintes.

November 30, 1782......................... Preliminary peace treaty between Britain and U.S. signed.

January 20, 1783 .... Preliminary treaty among Britain and Spain and France signed.

Glossary

American Prohibitory Act (1775): Parliamentary legislation that outlawed trade with America and effectively declared war on the American colonies.

Articles of Confederation: The preliminary constitution for the United States devised by the Continental Congress in 1776 but not ratified until 1781.

artillery: Refers to large-bore weaponry requiring service by a crew of gunners, and including field artillery (light direct-aim artillery for use in combat with infantry, mounted on wheeled carriages, and firing solid shot and grape or canister), siege artillery (heavy direct-aim artillery used in semi-permanent emplacements to bombard enemy fortifications), mortars (heavy high-trajectory artillery for siege use), howitzers (light high-trajectory artillery for field use), and naval artillery (direct-aim artillery mounted on roller-carriages for use on board warships), referred to commonly simply as "guns."

bayonet: Eighteen-inch, triangular-bladed edged weapon, attached to the muzzle of a musket with a socket, effectively converting the musket into a pike; the decisive weapon in battlefield combat in the 18th century.

blockade: Imposed by a navy on an enemy's ports, with warships preventing the entrance or departure of vessels.

brigade: An association of three or more regiments, commanded by a brigadier general.

cavalry: Soldiers mounted on horses for combat or scouting purposes; sometimes used as the force employed on fleeing or routed infantry to complete their disintegration; organized as heavy cavalry (for combat), light cavalry (scouting and pursuit), or dragoons.

column: The deployment of a unit with a narrow front and long files stretching behind; used for road movement or quick attack movement on a battlefield.

commissary general: Staff officer responsible for feeding and provisioning an army.

company: The smallest organizational unit of an army, numbering between 30 and 50 men.

Continental Congress: The joint directors of the colonial war of independence, composed of delegates from all the rebel colonies.

division: An association of two of more brigades, under the command of a major general.

dragoons: Heavy cavalry, armed with both sabers and carbines, able to fight as mounted shock troops or as dismounted skirmishers.

flank: The exposed right and left edges of a line or column of soldiers.

flotilla: A small collection of ships.

forage master: Staff officer responsible for feeding and provisioning the horses and livestock of an army.

frigate: A mid-sized warship, usually ship-rigged (three masts) and carrying between 36 and 50 naval guns.

garrison: Soldiers detailed to hold and occupy an outpost.

governor general: Officers representing British civil and military authority over Canada; delegated responsibilities to three lieutenants general.

grenadier: Originally referred to soldiers detailed to carry and use hand grenades in combat, but by the 18th century, the name for one company of each British regiment specializing in shock assault; normally distinguished by tall bearskin or half-crown hats.

habitants: French-speaking settlers within Britain's Canadian domains.

Hessians: Mercenaries hired by the British from the German principalities of Hesse-Cassel and Hesse-Hanau, but used generically to refer to any German units in British pay.

Highlanders: Describes the six regiments of Scottish soldiers recruited for British service from the Scottish Highlands.

inspector general: Staff officer responsible for the training of an army.

jäger: (German) Light infantry.

light infantry: Term applied to one company of each British regiment detailed and trained to act as skirmishers in front of a line of battle or as flankers to protect a column on the march; distinguished by short brimless caps.

line of battle: Deployment of a unit lengthwise into two or three lines, facing the enemy, in order to maximize delivery of firepower.

Loyalists: Term applied to Americans who remained loyal to the king or who served in militia companies supporting the British army; sometimes called "Tories" in derision.

magazine: Storage facility or depot for weapons, gunpowder, or supplies.

main army: The principal field force of the Continental army, serving in the mid-Atlantic region and commanded directly by Washington.

marines: Light infantry trained and detached to serve on board warships and responsible for the enforcement of ships' discipline, delivery of harassing fire by musket during ship-to-ship combat, and armed landings.

militia: Volunteer soldiers from the civil population, available for temporary call-up in the event of an emergency; frequently lacking in training and discipline necessary to undergo combat.

musket: Long-barreled personal firearm of the infantry, with a smooth (unrifled) bore, loaded from the muzzle, and discharged by means of a flintlock trigger system.

Northern army: The field force of the Continental army serving in upstate New York and Canada.

Olive Branch Petition (1775): The last gesture of conciliation offered by the Continental Congress to King George III.

Parliament: The governing legislature of the British Empire, composed of an elected House of Commons and a House of Lords; composed of the hereditary lords of the realm.

partisan: A guerilla fighter.

patronage: The system of discretionary appointments to government positions, or awards of government contracts, in the power of the king.

privateers: Privately owned ships commissioned by the Continental Congress under "letters of marque and reprisal" to harass or capture British commercial shipping.

purchase system: The principal mechanism by which British officers obtained commissions in the British army; literally, by paying a fixed amount of money.

quartermaster general: Staff officer responsible for supplying an army with equipment and clothing.

redoubt: A fort constructed by throwing up walls of earth and reinforcing them with wood or other materials.

regiment: The basic organizational unit of the British and Continental armies, consisting of 300–500 officers and men, subdivided into 8 to 10 companies.

regulars: Long-service (or "standing") professional soldiers; the British and Continental armies were "regulars," as opposed to militia, which were only called out in times of emergency; also referred to as "line" regiments.

republic: Any form of government that rests on popular consent or participation (hence, its derivation from the Latin, *res publica*), and that is not ruled by a monarchy, aristocracy, oligarchy, or dictatorship.

rifle: Long-barreled personal firearm featuring spiral grooves cut into the inside wall of the barrel to improve accuracy; because they were difficult to load, rifles were used by special units.

Seven Years' War: War between France and its allies and Britain and its allies from 1755–1762; also known as the "Great War for Empire" and, in America, as the "French and Indian War."

ship of the line: A full-sized warship, usually ship-rigged (three masts) and carrying between 64 and 104 naval guns; so-called from the standard naval deployment of these ships in combat in a line of battle.

skirmishers: Light infantry deployed as an open-order screen ahead of a regiment's battle line to harass enemy positions and clear enemy skirmishers out of the way of a regiment's attack.

sloop: A small, two-masted warship carrying between 4 and 20 naval guns.

Southern army: The field force of the Continental army serving in Georgia, Virginia, and the Carolinas.

staff: Officers detailed by the commander of the army to assist in carrying out support and executive responsibilities.

Whig: From the derisive term, *whiggamore* (a country yokel), applied to the British opposition party that was suspicious of a powerful monarchy and viewed itself as representing the virtue and independence of the "country," as opposed to the "court"; they tended to sympathize with the American rebels and eventually mounted sufficient opposition to force an end to the American war in 1782; opposed to Tories.

Biographical Notes

John Adams (1735–1826): Massachusetts lawyer, member of the Continental Congress, and diplomat. Took part in the Staten Island Peace Conference, represented the United States in France, and was a member of the team of negotiators that crafted the Treaty of Paris.

Samuel Adams (1722–1803): Massachusetts brewer and public official. Led Massachusetts opposition to Lt. Gov. Thomas Hutchinson and the Stamp Act, created the Massachusetts Committee of Correspondence, and was an early advocate for full American Independence from Britain in the Continental Congress.

William Alexander, Lord Stirling (1726–1783): American general. Prominent New York lawyer and merchant. He laid claim to the vacant earldom of Stirling, as the eldest male descendant of the first earl; although the House of Lords never recognized his claim, he continued to use the title throughout his life and was recognized as such in both Scotland and America. Appointed surveyor general of New Jersey, he was one of the founders of King's College (Columbia University). Appointed brigadier general by Congress in 1776, he distinguished himself in command of the Maryland Line at Long Island. Stirling was captured but exchanged and promoted to major general, and served under Washington at Trenton, Brandywine, Germantown, Monmouth, and Paulus Hook. Commanded the observation forces Washington left to secure New York during the Yorktown campaign.

Ethan Allen (1738–1789): American officer. Commanded a militia unit known as the "Green Mountain Boys" in the prewar land disputes between New York and New Hampshire over the "New Hampshire Grants" (Vermont). Allen led the Green Mountain Boys in a daring seizure of Fort Ticonderoga on May 10, 1775. Participated in Montgomery's expedition to Canada. Captured and then imprisoned in England, and not exchanged until 1778. He returned to border politics in Vermont and was even approached by the British to negotiate a separate peace that would make Vermont a British province.

Benedict Arnold (1741–1801): American general. Joined with Ethan Allen to capture Fort Ticonderoga, led the overland march on Canada, distinguished himself in the Saratoga campaign, and took command of the reoccupation of Philadelphia after the departure of the British in 1778. Convinced that he deserved better rewards for his service, he attempted to betray West Point to the British in 1780, and commanded British forces in Virginia in 1781.

John Barry (1745–1803): American naval officer. Commanded the brig *Lexington* in the first naval victory of the American navy over a British ship in 1776. His is the first name on the list of captains of the United States Navy.

John Burgoyne (1722–1792): British general and parliamentarian. Commissioned in the 13th Light Dragoons, then captain in 11th Dragoons, and finally lieutenant colonel, Coldstream Guards. Commissioned major general in 1772, sent to Boston in 1775, and commanded invasion of New York in 1777 that resulted in his surrender at Saratoga.

Sir Guy Carleton (1724–1808): British general and governor-general of Canada. Served under Wolfe at Quebec and appointed lieutenant governor of Canada in 1766. Appointed commander in chief in America in 1782 to succeed Sir Henry Clinton and supervised the British evacuation of New York in 1783.

Sir Henry Clinton (1738–1795): British general and third commander in chief in America during the Revolution. Commissioned major general in 1772 and sent to Boston, where he commanded part of an assault force at Bunker Hill. Served under Howe at Long Island and succeeded Howe as commander in chief in 1778. Supervised "Southern Strategy" of 1778–1781 but failed to support Cornwallis at Yorktown in 1781.

Charles Cornwallis, 1st Marquis and 2nd Earl Cornwallis (1738–1805): British general. Served under Clinton in first assault on Charleston; under Howe at Long Island, Brandywine, and Germantown; and again under Clinton as part of the "Southern Strategy." Victorious at Camden and Guildford Courthouse, he was forced to surrender his army at Yorktown in 1781.

John Dickinson (1732–1808): Pennsylvania and Delaware lawyer, political writer, member of the Continental Congress, and principal author of the Articles of Confederation.

Patrick Ferguson (1744–1780): British officer and pioneer of rifle tactics. Served in the West Indies and patented a breech-loading rifle, with which he equipped a battalion of riflemen for Howe's Philadelphia campaign. Wounded at Brandywine and assigned to Southern expedition in 1780, where he was killed at King's Mountain while attempting to cover Cornwallis's left flank with Tory militia.

Benjamin Franklin (1706–1790): American printer, publisher, scientist, and diplomat. Arrived penniless in Philadelphia from Boston in 1723 but built a publishing empire that allowed him to retire at age 48 to pursue scientific interests. Served as colonial agent in London until 1775 and served in the Second Continental Congress. Sent by Congress to represent the United States in France in 1776, he successfully negotiated both the French alliance and the Treaty of Paris.

Thomas Gage (1719/20–1787): British general and first commander in chief in America during the Revolution. Served in 44th Regiment under Braddock and commanded the 80th Regiment at Ticonderoga in French and Indian War. Served as military governor of Canada from 1760–1763, promoted to major general in 1761, and succeeded Amherst as commander in chief in America in 1763. Failed to deal effectively with American unrest leading up to Lexington and Concord, and was relieved of command in 1775 and returned to England.

Horatio Gates (1727–1806): American general. Served in 44th Regiment under Braddock in the French and Indian War and in the West Indies. Retired to a farm in Virginia in 1765. Selected by Washington to serve as adjutant general of the Continental army in 1775, and as commander of the Northern Department he forced the surrender of Burgoyne at Saratoga. He schemed to succeed Washington as American commander in chief, but his reputation was ruined by his disastrous defeat at Camden in 1780.

Marie-Joseph-Paul-Yves-Roch Gilbert du Motier, Marquis de Lafayette (1757–1834): French nobleman and volunteer. He arrived in South Carolina, June 13, 1777, and was commissioned major general by Congress, July 31. He served under Washington at Brandywine; designated to command the second Canada expedition, commanded Continental troops at Barren Hill, Monmouth, and Newport; and played a prominent role in Virginia in the campaigns leading to Yorktown. He participated in the French Revolution and revisited the United States on a triumphal tour in 1824–1826.

François-Joseph-Paul de Grasse-Rouville, Comte de Grasse (1722–1788): French admiral. He served in the French navy in the Seven Years' War, was promoted to commodore in 1778 and rear admiral in 1781, and commanded the French fleet cutting off Yorktown from the sea. Captured at the Battle of the Saintes, 1782, and became intermediary of Lord Shelburne in opening peace negotiations.

Nathanael Greene (1742–1786): American general. Originally brigadier general of Rhode Island militia, he was made brigadier general of Continental troops in 1775 and was held responsible for defeat at Fort Washington (1776). He had the confidence of Washington, however, and fought at Brandywine and Germantown, then served as Washington's quartermaster general at Valley Forge. Given command of the Southern Department in 1780, he conducted a wearing campaign against Cornwallis that eventually led to Cornwallis's surrender at Yorktown.

Alexander Hamilton (1757–1804): American officer. Born illegitimate in the West Indies, he entered King's College as a scholarship student in 1773 and organized a student militia company in 1775. He attracted attention for his handling of artillery at Long Island and White Plains and was attached to Washington's staff as secretary and aide-de-camp in 1777. He returned to field command in Hazen's Brigade in time to distinguish himself in leading the attacks on Redoubts 9 and 10 at Yorktown. He later served as Washington's secretary of the treasury from 1789–1795.

John Hancock (1737–1793): American merchant and politician. Graduated from Harvard in 1754 and together with Samuel Adams became principal figure of resistance to British authority in Massachusetts. He was the President of the Massachusetts Provincial Congress from 1774–1775 and president of the Second Continental Congress from 1775–1777.

Patrick Henry (1736–1799): Virginia legislator. The child of Scot immigrants to western Virginia, he began practicing law in 1760 and scored a notable success in his handling of the "Parson's Cause" in 1763. Elected to the House of Burgesses in 1765, where he opposed the Stamp Act and, in 1775, urged resistance to Lord Dunmore with the famous words "… give me liberty or give me death." Served briefly in the Second Continental Congress and commanded the Virginia state militia. Elected governor in 1776, and then again in 1784. Was a major force in the adoption of the Bill of Rights as the first 10 amendments to the U.S. Constitution.

Samuel Hood, 1st Viscount Hood (1724–1816): British admiral. Commanded HMS *Jamaica* in the French and Indian War and promoted to rear admiral in 1780 to serve under Rodney in the West Indies. Defeated and captured de Grasse at the Battle of the Saintes in 1782.

Richard Howe, 4th Viscount Howe (1726–1799): British admiral and naval commander in chief in America, brother of Sir William Howe. Entered the navy at age 14 and rose to vice admiral by 1775. Given overall naval command in America in 1776 and served as peace commissioner. Declined to serve further under Germain or Lord Sandwich and returned home. He reassumed command in the navy in 1782 and relieved the British garrison of Gibraltar.

Sir William Howe (1729–1814): British general and second commander in chief in America during the Revolution, younger brother of Admiral Richard Howe. Served under Wolfe in the storming of Quebec (1759) and as adjutant general in the capture of Havana (1760). He was promoted to major general in 1772 and sent, despite his political sympathies with the Americans, to serve under Thomas Gage in 1775. He was in tactical command at Bunker Hill (1775) and succeeded to commander in chief in 1776. Although repeatedly victorious at Long Island, Brandywine, and Germantown, he was unable to destroy the Continental army and was relieved at his own request in 1778.

Thomas Jefferson (1743–1826): Author of the American Declaration of Independence and third president of the U.S. Elected to represent Virginia in the Second Continental Congress. His reputation as the author of the *Summary View of the Rights of British America* (1774) led to appointment to the committee responsible for drafting the Declaration of Independence. The subsequent document was almost entirely from Jefferson's own pen. He served in the Virginia House of Delegates and was chosen governor to succeed Patrick Henry in 1779. But his term was clouded by charges that he had fled in the face of British raiding parties in Virginia in 1781. Jefferson was elected to the Confederation Congress in 1783 and wrote legislation creating an American currency and a Northwest Ordinance, banning slavery in the Northwest Territories.

John Paul Jones (1747–1792): American naval officer. Born in Scotland as John Paul, he was apprenticed to a shipowner at age 12 and rose to become a merchant captain until he was charged with the flogging death of a seaman and the killing of a mutineer. He immigrated to America and took the surname Jones. In 1775 he was commissioned as first lieutenant on the Continental navy's first ship, the *Alfred*. Jones was promoted to captain and given command of the *Ranger*, with which he raided the English coast, and then took command of the ex-French vessel *Bonhomme Richard*, with which he won a lopsided victory over HMS *Serapis* on September 23, 1779. After the Revolution, he served in the navy of Catherine the Great and died penniless in Paris. His remains were reburied at the U.S. Naval Academy in 1913.

Johann de Kalb, Baron de Kalb (1721–1780): French and American general. Served in the French army during the Seven Years' War and acted as a French spy in North America. Volunteered to serve with Continental army with Lafayette in 1777 and was commissioned major general. Mortally wounded at the Battle of Camden (1780).

Henry Knox (1750–1806): American general and chief of artillery. Originally the owner of a Boston bookstore, Knox read widely in military matters, and after serving at Bunker Hill, Washington appointed him chief of the Continental artillery. He successfully manhandled the artillery captured at Fort Ticonderoga through the winter snow to Boston, where the threat of Knox's guns forced the British to evacuate Boston. He was appointed brigadier general in 1776 and served as one of Washington's most faithful and stalwart staffers. He was then appointed major general in 1782 and succeeded Washington as commander of the Continental army in 1783. Later he served as secretary of war during Washington's presidency (1789–1794).

Tadeusz (Thaddeus) Andrzej Bonawentura Kosciuszko (1746–1817): Minor Polish nobleman and American general. He arrived as a volunteer in America in 1776 and designed the Delaware River fortification. Commissioned colonel of engineers by Congress, he fought at Saratoga and constructed the defense of West Point. He fought under Greene in the Southern campaign and after promotion to brigadier general in 1784, he left to lead a defense of Poland against Russian invasion. He supported the French Revolution, led an abortive uprising in Poland, and returned to America in 1797.

Henry Laurens (1724–1792): President of the Continental Congress. Successful Charleston merchant and agent for transatlantic slave trading, he was elected to the South Carolina Provincial Congress in 1775 and participated in the defense of Charleston in 1776. Elected to the Continental Congress, he succeeded John Hancock as president in 1777, in which he rebuffed attempts to undercut Washington. Sent as Congressional agent in 1779 to negotiate with the Netherlands, and on this mission, he was intercepted at sea by a British vessel and imprisoned for treason in the Tower of London. He was exchanged in 1781 for Earl Cornwallis and joined the team of peace negotiators in London. His son, John Laurens, was one of Washington's aides and his son-in-law, David Ramsay, was an early historian of the Revolution.

Charles Lee (1731–1782): American general. Originally an ensign in the 44th Foot, he served as part of Braddock's expedition in the French and Indian War, fought at Ticonderoga, and was part of the expedition that captured Montreal. Appointed major of the 103rd Foot in 1761, he was retired when the regiment disbanded in 1763, and served in the Polish army until moving to America in 1773. He was commissioned as major general by the Continental Congress in 1775 and led a successful defense of Charleston in 1776. He was suspected of scheming to supplant Washington, and when he was captured in a daring British raid at Basking Ridge, New Jersey, on December 13, 1776, he freely gave advice to the Howe brothers on how to end the war. Exchanged in April 1778, he rejoined the Continental army, only to arouse Washington's ire for mishandling his troops at Monmouth, and was court-martialed for his conduct toward Washington afterward.

Francis Marion (c. 1732–1795): American partisan leader. A delegate to the South Carolina Provincial Congress in 1775, he participated in the defense of Charleston as a captain in the 2nd South Carolina, which he eventually rose to command. He participated in an unsuccessful assault on Savannah in 1779, and after the fall of Charleston in 1780, he conducted wide-ranging partisan raids against the British and acquired the reputation of "The Swamp Fox." He also commanded the combined Carolina militia forces under Greene at Eutaw Springs in 1781.

Daniel Morgan (1735–1802): American general. Born in Pennsylvania, he moved to Virginia in 1753 and served as a teamster in Braddock's expedition in the French and Indian War and as a militia captain in Pontiac's Rebellion and Lord Dunmore's War. He was commissioned captain of a Virginia rifle company in 1775 and served with distinction in Montgomery's assault on Quebec, where he was captured. After an exchange, he took command of the 11th Virginia and was authorized by Washington to recruit a battalion of rifle-armed Continental "rangers." He fought at Saratoga, served in Woodford's Brigade at Valley Forge, and fought at Monmouth. He briefly resigned his commission in a dispute over rank, but rejoined the army after the disaster at Camden in 1780, and distinguished himself at Cowpens (1781).

William Moultrie (1730–1805): American general. Son of an English physician, he grew up in South Carolina and rose to become a captain in the provincial militia. He was commissioned colonel of the 2nd South Carolina and distinguished himself during the British attack on Charleston in 1776 in command of the palmetto-log fort that was given his name. The second

British expedition against Charleston (1780) resulted in the surrender of the city and Moultrie's capture. He was exchanged in 1782, and was the last officer promoted to major general in the Continental army.

John Peter Gabriel Muhlenberg (1746–1807): Lutheran and Episcopalian clergyman and American general. He served congregations in Virginia from 1772–1775, but was invited by Washington to take up a colonelcy in the Continental army, and recruited 300 of his congregation as the 8th Virginia. Served in the defense of Charleston (1776), Brandywine, and Germantown, where he rose to brigadier general and commanded 1st, 5th, 6th, 9th, and 13th Virginia. He served under Wayne at Stony Point, under von Steuben in the Southern campaign, and under Lafayette at Yorktown.

Sir Frederick North, Lord North and 2nd Earl of Guilford (1732–1792): He won election to parliament in 1754 and was chancellor of the exchequer (1767–1782) and opposed concessions to the Americans. A favorite of George III, he bears principal political responsibility for triggering the American Revolution and for prolonging the war. By 1778, he had given up hope of victory in America but yielded to the demands of the king to remain in office until 1782.

Enoch Poor (1736–1780): American general. A shipbuilder and cabinetmaker, he was elected to the New Hampshire provincial congress and named colonel of the 2nd New Hampshire in 1775. He served under Washington at Trenton and Princeton, and then, as a brigadier general, commanded a brigade at Saratoga. He was part of the encampment at Valley Forge and saw action at Monmouth and in Sullivan's Iroquois expedition in 1779.

Paul Revere (1735–1818): American artisan and political organizer. Beginning with the Stamp Act protests in Boston, Revere took a leading role in rallying fellow artisans and "mechanics" to resistance of British imperial policies, and served as a courier between colonial committees of correspondence. His most famous ride was on the evening of April 18–19, 1775, when he slipped out of Boston ahead of a British expedition to warn the county militias and secure the escape of John Hancock and Samuel Adams. He served in various capacities in the militia during the Revolution, none of them happy, and in 1782 he was court-martialed (but acquitted) for his conduct in the Penobscot River expedition (1779). After the Revolution, he went on to great commercial success, especially as the inventor of a process for rolling sheet copper.

Sir George Rodney, Baron Rodney (1719–1792): British admiral. Participated in the capture of Louisbourg during the French and Indian War and conducted a successful naval campaign in the West Indies (1761–1762). Promoted to admiral in 1778, he was appointed naval commander in chief in the West Indies and defeated the French at Cape St. Vincent (1780) and participated in the defeat of the French at the Saintes (1782).

George Sackville, Lord Germain and Viscount Sackville (1716–1785): British soldier and secretary of state for America. Court-martialed for disobedience of orders at Minden (1759), he inherited the property and title from Lady Elizabeth Germain and rebuilt his reputation as a politician through firm resistance to the demands of the colonies. When he succeeded Lord Dartmouth as secretary of state for America, he attempted to overmanage the course of the war in America and was noted for his truculence in refusing any form of compromise. He resigned in February 1782 when the surrender at Yorktown made it clear that no hope remained of military victory in America.

Philip John Schuyler (1733–1804): Prominent New York landholder and American general. As a leading member of the old Dutch ascendancy, he was elected to the state legislature in 1768 and in 1775. The Continental Congress appointed Schuyler as a major general and he served as the principal supply officer for Montgomery's Quebec campaign. Given command of the Northern Department, he ordered the evacuation of Fort Ticonderoga in the face of Burgoyne's invasion in 1777 and was relieved of command (although he stayed in the field to serve under his replacement, Horatio Gates, and join with Benedict Arnold as one of the principal architects of the Saratoga victory). He was acquitted of charges of incompetence by court-martial in 1778. He was elected to represent New York in the Continental Congress in 1779. His daughter, Elizabeth, married Alexander Hamilton.

John Sullivan (1740–1795): American general. Commissioned as brigadier general by the Continental Congress in 1775, he briefly commanded the Northern Department and was captured at Long Island (1776), then exchanged. He served under Washington at Trenton, Princeton, Brandywine, and Germantown. He failed in the attempt to retake Newport in 1778 and conducted a campaign against the Iroquois in 1779. He was also governor of New Hampshire from 1785–1790.

Thomas Sumter, "The Carolina Gamecock" (1734–1832): American partisan officer. Served under Braddock in the French and Indian War and settled in South Carolina in 1765. Appointed captain of mounted rangers at the beginning of the Revolution, he became best known for his command of partisans during the Southern campaign. He was the last surviving American general of the Revolution.

Banastre Tarleton (1754–1833): British officer. Commissioned in the 1st Dragoon Guards in 1775, he volunteered for service in America and led the 16th Light Dragoons in capture of Charles Lee (1776). Appointed to command the British Legion in 1778, he served under Cornwallis in the Southern campaign and acquired an unsavory reputation for taking no prisoners. Defeated at Cowpens (1781), he surrendered with Cornwallis at Yorktown. He entered Parliament in 1790 and was knighted in 1820.

James Mitchell Varnum (1748–1789): American general. Graduate of Brown and successful lawyer, he responded to the call of Paul Revere and joined the militia besieging Boston in 1775. He was commissioned colonel of the 1st Rhode Island and then promoted to brigadier general. Led defense of Forts Mercer and Mifflin in 1777. Resigned commission in 1779 and became major general of Rhode Island militia. He served in the Confederation Congress from 1780–1782 and 1786–1787.

Jean Baptiste Donatien de Vimeur, Comte de Rochambeau (1725–1807): French general and commander of French expeditionary force in North America. Arrived at Newport on July 10, 1780, and cooperated with Washington in the siege of New York City and the Yorktown campaign. Retiring in 1791 as a Marshal of France, he narrowly avoided the guillotine in the French Revolution.

Wilhelm von Knyphausen, Baron Knyphausen (1716–1800): Prussian general and senior commanding officer of German troops in British service in America. He commanded a division of German mercenaries under Sir William Howe at Long Island, Fort Washington, and Brandywine, and under Sir Henry Clinton at Monmouth.

Friedrich Wilhelm Ludolf Gerhard Augustin von Steuben, Baron von Steuben (1730–1794): Prussian officer and inspector general of the Continental army. A minor staff officer in the Prussian army and court chamberlain of Hohenzollern-Hechingen, he parlayed his meager military credentials into a mythic reputation as a Prussian lieutenant general and was accepted by Congress as a volunteer for the Continental army. He turned out to be an enormously effective drillmaster and rewrote the Continental army's basic tactics during the Valley Forge encampment. Designated inspector general in 1778, he served as a staff officer at Monmouth, and commanded one of Washington's divisions at Yorktown.

Charles Watson-Wentworth, 2nd Marquis of Rockingham (1730–1782): A leading critic of George III in Parliament, he had served as prime minister for the repeal of the Stamp Act (1765–1766) and was a vocal opponent of the use of military force to subdue the colonies. With the fall of Lord North as prime minister in 1782, Rockingham once again became prime minister, but only for four months before his death.

Anthony Wayne, "Mad Anthony" (1745–1796): American general. A tanner and surveyor, he participated in the first Canadian expedition (1775–1776) and was appointed brigadier general under Washington in 1777. Fought at Brandywine, Paoli, Germantown, Monmouth, and Stony Point, and served under Steuben in Virginia in 1781. Named senior general of the U.S. Army in 1792 and successfully cleared pro-British Indians from the Northwest Territory at the Battle of Fallen Timbers in 1794.

Bibliography

General Histories of the American Revolution

Alden, John R. *A History of the American Revolution.* New York: Knopf, 1969. The best overall survey of the Revolution, particularly in its military aspects.

Conway, Thomas. The *War of American Independence, 1775–1783.* New York: Edward Arnold, 1995. Written from a British perspective, Conway includes much valuable material on the extended frontiers of the American war in Europe and the West Indies.

Higginbotham, Don. *The War of American Independence: Military Attitudes, Policies, and Practice, 1763–1789.* New York: Macmillan, 1971. A detailed, although somewhat chaotic, interpretation of the command dynamics of the Continental army.

Mackesy, Piers. *The War for America, 1775–1783.* Lincoln: University of Nebraska Press, 1993. A difficult and diffuse book, written brilliantly but haphazardly, from the British perspective, but containing priceless coverage of British command decision making.

Wood, Gordon. *The American Revolution: A History.* New York: Knopf, 2002. The finest short survey of the Revolution, although more oriented toward social and political issues than military ones.

Collections of Primary Documents

Boyd, Julian P., ed. *The Papers of Thomas Jefferson.* Princeton: Princeton University Press, 1950–2006, 21 vols. The definitive edition of Jefferson's papers.

Conrad, Dennis M., Roger N. Parks, and Martha J. King, eds. *The Papers of General Nathanael Greene.* Chapel Hill: University of North Carolina Press, 1976–2005. An ambitious edition of all of Greene's letters and documents; volumes 7–9 cover his service in the Southern campaign.

Dann, John C., ed. *The Revolution Remembered: Eyewitness Accounts of the War for Independence.* Chicago: University of Chicago Press, 1980. An anthology of reminiscences of American soldiers who fought in the various campaigns and battles of the Revolution, many of them drawn from pension application records.

Davies, K. G., ed. *Documents of the American Revolution, 1770–1783. (Colonial Office Series).* Dublin: Irish University Press, 1975–1981), 21 vols. A vast but indispensable collection of the pertinent British military and political documents on the conduct of the war, including Germain's correspondence and his generals' campaign and battle reports.

Ewald, Johann. *Diary of the American War: A Hessian Journal.* Edited by Joseph P. Tustin. New Haven: Yale University Press, 1979. The journal of Capt. Johann Ewald of the Hessian jägers, a humane, literate, sometimes bemused description of his service in every campaign from Trenton to Yorktown.

Foner, Philip, ed. *The Life and Major Writings of Thomas Paine.* Secaucus, NJ: Citadel Press, 1948; reprint, 1974. A single-volume compilation of Paine's most controversial publications.

Ford, W. C., ed. *Journals of the Continental Congress.* Washington DC: Government Printing Office, 1904–1937. 34 vols. The minutes of the proceedings of the First and Second Continental Congresses, up till the Congress's supersession by the new federal Congress under the 1787 Constitution. Also available online at http://memory.loc.gov/ammem/amlaw/lwjc.html.

Gruber, Ira D., ed. *John Peebles' American War: The Diary of a Scottish Grenadier, 1776–1782.* Mechanicsburg, PA: Stackpole, 1998. Unlike Capt. Ewald's journal, which was rewritten years after the events he describes, Capt. Peebles's diary is hurried, informative, observant, and contemporary, and allows a view of the Revolution through the eyes of a British junior officer.

Hutchinson, Peter O., ed. *The Diary and Letters of His Excellency, Thomas Hutchinson.* 1884; New York: Ames reprint, 1973, 2 vols. A chronicle of frustration from the ultimate Loyalist.

Jensen, Merrill, ed. *Tracts of the American Revolution, 1763–1776.* Indianapolis: Hackett, 1967. A volume in the classic Bobbs-Merrill "American Heritage Series," this volume collects 17 principal political arguments made by American writers for (and against) independence (including Paine's *Common Sense*).

Macdonald, William, ed. *Select Charters and Other Documents Illustrative of American History, 1606–1775.* New York: Macmillan, 1899. Although this collection of 80 charters, bills, and decrees includes the major documents of all the colonies, from their founding, the last 25 form the principal documents leading up to the Revolution, concluding with the Prohibitory Bill.

Ross, Charles, ed. *Correspondence of Charles, First Marquis Cornwallis.* London: J. Murray, 1859, 3 vols. A venerable but extremely handy collection of Cornwallis's correspondence, including his service in America (volume two), which undermines the stereotype of Cornwallis as a brutal incompetent.

Scheer, George F. and Hugh Rankin. *Rebels and Redcoats: The American Revolution Through the Eyes of Those Who Fought and Lived It.* Cleveland: World Publishing, 1957. Like the Dann collection, this brings together the personal accounts of British soldiers on campaign in the Revolution.

Sparks, Jared, ed. *Writings of George Washington.* Boston: John M. Russell, 1834–1837, 12 vols. There are numerous anthologies and collections of the writings of George Washington; I have chosen to list the Sparks edition because it is neither too brief, nor so exhaustingly endless as the University of Virginia *Papers of George Washington* edition; volumes 3–8 cover the Revolutionary years.

Syrett, Harold C., ed. *The Papers of Alexander Hamilton.* New York: Columbia University Press, 1961, 27 vols. A thorough assemblage of Hamilton's letters, reports, and papers; volumes 1–2 cover his service in the Revolution.

Willcox, W. B., ed. *The American Rebellion: Sir Henry Clinton's Narrative of His Campaigns, 1775–1782.* New Haven: Yale University Press, 1954. Clinton's self-justifying account of his conduct of the war as British commander in chief in North America.

Campaign and Battle Histories—Biographies—Social and Political Histories

Alden, John R. *General Gage in America.* Baton Rouge: Louisiana State University Press, 1948. Sympathetically underscores the dilemma of a British officer charged with subduing a people whom he had lived with, almost as one of them.

Arnold, Isaac Newton. *The Life of Benedict Arnold.* Chicago: Jansen, McClurg, 1880. A comprehensive 19th century biography, by a veteran politician and descendant of Arnold.

Babits, Lawrence E. *A Devil of a Whipping: The Battle of Cowpens.* Chapel Hill: University of North Carolina Press, 1998. A phenomenally detailed account of Morgan's defeat of Tarleton, along with debunking of several myths about the battle.

Bailyn, Bernard. *Ideological Origins of the American Revolution* Cambridge, MA: Harvard University Press, 1967. A landmark study of the political ideas that moved Americans to their Revolution, concentrating on the broad heritage of Whig, Puritan, and practical sources of opposition to Parliamentary centralization of power.

Benninghoff, Herman O. *The Brilliance of Yorktown: A March of History, 1781 Command and Control, Allied Style*. Gettysburg: Thomas Publications, 2006. A careful analysis of the planning and organization of Washington and Rochambeau's march to Virginia.

Billias, George Athan, ed. *George Washington's Generals and Opponents: Their Exploits and Leadership*. New York: William Morrow and Co., 1969. An outstanding collection of biographical essays on the principal British and American commanders of the war.

Bodle, Wayne. *The Valley Forge Winter: Civilians and Soldiers at War*. University Park: Penn State University Press, 2002. A thorough description of the 1777–1778 Continental army encampment at Valley Forge, with particular emphasis on the failure of Continental logistics and the explosion of several popular stereotypes.

Borick, Carl P. *A Gallant Defense: The Siege of Charleston, 1780*. Columbia: University of South Carolina Press, 2003. A meticulous description of Charleston's siege, with a preliminary account of the failed 1776 British attack and a particularly well-paced retelling of Sir Henry Clinton's 1780 rematch.

Bowler, R. Arthur. *Logistics and the Failure of the British Army in America, 1775–1783*. Princeton: Princeton University Press, 1975. Logistics is a dry subject, and this is a dry book, but it is the most thorough examination of the weak link in British plans to conquer America.

Brumwell, Stephen. *Redcoats: The British Soldier and the War in the Americas, 1755–1763*. Cambridge: Cambridge University Press, 2002. A study of the life and experiences of British soldiers in America through the French and Indian Wars; a useful preliminary to understanding British garrison life in America in the pre-Revolution decade.

Buchanan, John. *The Road to Guilford Courthouse: The American Revolution in the Carolinas*. New York: Wiley, 1997. A rollicking and sprawling account of the Revolution in the Carolina colonies, with forceful and controversial evaluations of a number of the major American players.

———, *The Road to Valley Forge: How Washington Built the Army that Won the Revolution*. New York: Wiley, 2004. A fine account of how Washington constructed the Continental army in the years 1776 and 1777.

Buckley, Roger Norman. *The British Army in the West Indies: Society and the Military in the Revolutionary War*. Gainesville, FL: University of

Florida Press, 1998. A useful comparison study of a British garrison society, this time in the West Indies.

Carp, E. Wayne. *To Starve the Army at Pleasure: Continental Army Administration and American Political Culture, 1775–1783*. Chapel Hill, NC: University of North Carolina Press, 1984. A sharply focused study on the failures and frustrations of the Continental army's leadership with the civilian politicians who were supposed to supply them.

Chartrand, René. *The French Army in the American War of Independence*. Oxford, UK: Osprey, 1991. A "Men-at-Arms" short book on the reforms and reorganization of the French army after the Seven Years' War, with illustrations of the uniforms and weapons used by Rochambeau's regiments in America.

Clark, J. C. D. *The Language of Liberty, 1660–1832*. Cambridge, UK: Cambridge University Press, 1994. An ambitious and complex study of the key terms and ideas used by the American Revolutionaries, connecting them particularly to nonconformist religion in England in the 18th century.

Countryman, Edward. *A People in Revolution: The American Revolution and Political Society in New York, 1760–1790*. Baltimore: Johns Hopkins University Press, 1981. A detailed study of the social tensions generated by the Revolution, especially among the landed gentry of the Hudson Valley and their restless tenants who often sought to ally themselves with the British in order to throw off gentry rule.

Davis, David Brion. *Inhuman Bondage: The Rise and Fall of Slavery in the New World*. New York: Oxford University Press, 2006. Davis's survey is a comprehensive account of the whole history of slavery in the Americas, with two chapters that concentrate on the experience of slave refugees during the Revolution.

Dell, Jonathan R. *The French Navy and American Independence: A Study of Arms and Diplomacy, 1774–1787*. Princeton: Princeton University Press, 1975. Examines the contribution of the French navy to the American victory in the Revolution, along with valuable material on the reconstruction of the French navy after the Seven Years' War and the challenge it offered to the Royal Navy in home waters.

Desjardins, Thomas A. *Through A Howling Wilderness: Benedict Arnold's March to Quebec, 1775*. New York: St. Martin's Press, 2006. A popular account of Benedict Arnold's overland expedition from the coast of Maine to Quebec, climaxing with the ill-fated attack on Quebec.

Dickinson, H. T., ed. *Britain and the American Revolution*. London: Longman, 1988. A collection of essays on the impact of the American Revolution in the British Isles, with a particularly good chapter on Parliamentary opposition to the American war.

Ellis, Joseph J. *His Excellency George Washington*. New York: Vintage, 2004. A popular one-volume overview of the life of Washington, concentrating mostly on his post-Revolutionary career.

Ferling, John E. *Almost a Miracle: The American Victory in the War of Independence*. New York: Oxford University Press, 2007. A thick, readable, and clear-as-crystal survey of the Revolution, with the primary emphasis on the campaigns, and an unusually helpful conclusion on the post-Revolution dissolution of the Continental army.

Fischer, David Hackett. *Paul Revere's Ride*. New York: Oxford University Press, 1994. A marvelous and detailed narrative of the most famous ride in American history, stressing how much of the American response was more organized and "regular" than popular perceptions of the minutemen usually convey.

———. *Washington's Crossing*. New York: Oxford University Press, 2004. Like *Paul Revere's Ride*, a thorough and well-written account of the Battle of Trenton, in which Washington is the unquestioned master of the hour and the embodiment of the Revolution's cause.

Fleming, Thomas J. *Now We Are Enemies: The Story of Bunker Hill*. New York: St. Martins, 1960. Still the best retelling of the Battle of Bunker Hill, well narrated, with good maps and a firm command of the primary sources from both British and American participants.

———.*Washington's Secret War: The Hidden History of Valley Forge*. New York: Harper Collins/First Smithsonian, 2005. A popular account of the Valley Forge encampment, with the focus on Washington's political skill in outmaneuvering his critics in Congress and his rivals in uniform.

Flexner, James Thomas. *George Washington in the American Revolution, 1775–1783*. Boston: Little, Brown, and Co., 1968. The second volume in Flexner's multi-volume classic biography of Washington, masterfully well written.

Fowler, William M. *Rebels Under Sail: The American Navy during the American Revolution*. New York: Scribner, 1976. A fine popular narrative of the creation and combats of the Continental navy, particularly strong on the Continental navy's first expeditions to the Bahamas.

Freeman, Douglas Southall. *Washington*. Abbreviated by Richard Harwell. New York: Scribner, 1995. Freeman's seven volumes are still the go-to biography of Washington, but for our purposes are wisely distilled here down to a single useful volume.

Furneaux, Rupert. *Saratoga: The Decisive Battle*. London: Allen and Unwin, 1971. A fine account from the British viewpoint, using British source materials.

Gipson, Lawrence Henry. *The Triumphant Empire: The Rumbling of the Coming Storm, 1766–1770*. New York: Knopf, 1967. Volume 12 in Gipson's series on the British Empire before the Revolution; covers the events leading up to the Boston Massacre.

———. *The Triumphant Empire: Thunder-Clouds Gather in the West, 1763–1766*. New York: Knopf, 1967. Volume 11 in Gipson's magisterial survey of politics in Britain and in each of the 13 mainland colonies in the decade before the Revolution; covers the Stamp Act and its repeal.

Golway, Terry. *Washington's General: Nathanael Greene and the Triumph of the American Revolution*. New York: Henry Holt, 2005. A splendid biography of Greene, emphasizing both his considerable organizational skills but also the unhappy, thin-skinned temperament that cost him many of the advances he would otherwise have gained.

Greene, Jack P. *Pursuits of Happiness: The Social Development of Early Modern British Colonies and the Formation of American Culture*. Chapel Hill: University of North Carolina, 1988. Greene's thesis is that the American colonies were founded as decisive breaks with British culture in the 17th century but were gradually moving toward more and more assimilation to British cultural values until the Revolution intervened.

Greene, J. P. and J. R. Pole, eds. *Colonial British America: Essays in the New History of the Early Modern Era*. Baltimore: Johns Hopkins University Press, 1984. A state-of-the-art survey of the major topics of historical interest in the history of the British North American colonies, with essays by major historians on each topic.

Gross, Robert A. *The Minutemen and Their World*. New York: Hill and Wang, 1976. A delightfully minute social history of Concord, Massachusetts, and the British raid that brought a revolution to its doorsteps.

Hammon, Neal O. and Richard Taylor. *Virginia's Western War, 1775–1786*. Mechanicsburg, PA: Stackpole, 2002. A diffuse and not entirely well-organized narrative of the British-inspired warfare on Virginia's Kentucky frontier, but teeming with detail.

Isaac, Rhys. *The Transformation of Virginia, 1740–1790*. Chapel Hill: University of North Carolina Press, 1982. A mold-breaking analysis of the culture of colonial Virginia, and why its leadership was moved to gamble on the movement to independence.

Jensen, Merrill. *The Articles of Confederation: An Interpretation of the Social-Constitutional History of the American Revolution, 1774–1781*. Madison, WI: University of Wisconsin Press, 1959. The most thorough analysis of the creation and content of the first American "constitution," with vast attention to the quarrels that delayed its ratification and with a surprising amount of sympathy for the distrust of elite government that it seemed to embody.

———. *The Founding of a Nation: A History of the American Revolution, 1763–1776*. New York: Oxford University Press, 1968. An early "social history" of American motives for resistance to British imperial authority in the decade leading up to independence.

Johnston, Henry P. *The Yorktown Campaign and the Surrender of Cornwallis*. New York: Harper, 1881. A classic account of the campaign and siege of Yorktown; despite its age, its account of the armies and the progress of the siege is more detailed and useful than many modern versions.

Ketchum, Richard M. *Saratoga: Turning Point of America's Revolutionary War*. New York: Henry Holt, 1997. A popular history of the Saratoga campaign, covering the pre-invasion American preparations, the capture of Ticonderoga, and the British debacles at Bennington and Bemis Heights.

———. *Victory at Yorktown: The Campaign that Won the Revolution*. New York: Henry Holt, 2004. Another popular battle history by the Ketchum, although only the second half of the book really concentrates on Yorktown.

Kurtz, Stephen and James Hutson, eds. *Essays on the American Revolution*. New York: W. W. Norton and Co., 1973. An important collection of essays, reinterpreting many of the customary understandings of the Revolution, including an essay by John Shy on the military experience.

Mahan, Alfred Thayer. *The Major Operations of the Navies in the War of American Independence*. 1913; reprint: Gloucestershire, UK: Nonsuch Publishing, 2006. Written by one of the great naval strategists of the "dreadnought" era, it remains a fabulously detailed and authoritative account of the major actions of the American, French, and British navies in the Revolution.

Maier, Pauline. *American Scripture: Making the Declaration of Independence*. New York: Vintage, 1997. A detailed analysis of the sources Jefferson drew upon in composing the Declaration of Independence, and the document's subsequent reputation as a touchstone definition of American democracy.

Main, Jackson Turner. *The Sovereign States, 1775–1783*. New York: New Viewpoints, 1973. A skillful political history of the American colonies under the rule of Congress and the state governments.

May, Robin. *The British Army in North America, 1775–1783*. Oxford: Osprey, 1974. An early volume in the "Men-at-Arms" series of short illustrated books, concentrating on the arms, uniforms, and equipment of the British troops in the Revolutionary War.

————. *Wolfe's Army*. Oxford: Osprey, 1974. Another volume in the "Men-at-Arms" series, this time focused on the British army in North America during the Seven Years' War.

McConnell, Michael N. *Army and Empire: British Soldiers on the American Frontier, 1758–1775*. Lincoln: University of Nebraska Press, 2004. A fine analysis of the composition and personal lives of British soldiers stationed in America up to the brink of the Revolution.

McCusker, John J. and Russell R. Menard. *The Economy of British America, 1607–1789*. Chapel Hill: University of North Carolina Press, 1991. A hefty but absolutely authoritative volume on the colonial economy, teeming with data and insights on the struggle of Americans to stabilize their place in the overall imperial economy.

McGuire, Thomas J. *Battle of Paoli*. Mechanicsburg, PA: Stackpole, 2000. A vigorous narrative of the daring night-time attack on Anthony Wayne's Pennsylvania Continentals; benefits from a detailed knowledge of the geography of the battlefield.

————. *The Philadelphia Campaign: Brandywine and the Fall of Philadelphia*. Mechanicsburg, PA: Stackpole, 2006. The first volume in a large-scale account of the British campaign to capture Philadelphia, focusing in this case on the defeat at Brandywine. Probably the most exhaustive account of the Brandywine battle ever written.

Miller, Nathan. *Sea of Glory: The Continental Navy Fights for Independence, 1775–1783*. New York: Donald McKay, 1974. A popular history of the formation and personalities of the Continental navy.

Milsop, John. *Continental Infantryman of the American Revolution*. Oxford: Osprey, 2004. Another in the illustrated series of "Men-at-Arms" books, concentrating on the uniforms and equipment of the Continental army.

Morris, Richard B. *The Peacemakers: The Great Powers and American Independence*. New York: Harper and Row, 1965. A venerable but still vital account of the complexities of the peace-making process, from the establishment of American representatives in Europe to the Treaty of Paris.

Nash, Gary B. *The Unknown American Revolution: The Unruly Birth of Democracy and the Struggle to Create America*. New York: Viking, 2005. A somewhat garrulous survey of the "losers" of the Revolution, with the conclusion that the Revolution represented a struggle for genuine democracy that was quashed by American elites.

———. *The Urban Crucible: Social Change, Political Consciousness, and the Origins of the American Revolution*. Cambridge, MA: Harvard University Press, 1979. Surveys the breakdown of social and economic life in three major colonial port cities and draws attention to the role these disruptions played in preparing Americans for revolution.

Nelson, Paul David. *Anthony Wayne: Soldier of the Early Republic*. Bloomington: Indiana University Press, 1985. Outstanding biographical survey of "mad Anthony," whose post-Revolutionary career was almost as legendary as his Revolutionary one.

Norton, Mary Beth. *The British Americans: The Loyalist Exiles in England, 1774–1789*. Boston: Little, Brown, 1972. A sprightly and sympathetic account of the agony of the American Loyalists, first to influence British policy toward vigorous suppression of the Revolution, and then to wring restitution from the hands of an unsympathetic imperial government.

O'Shaughnessy, Andrew Jackson. *An Empire Divided: The American Revolution and the British Caribbean*. Philadelphia: University of Pennsylvania Press, 2000. Examines how the British West Indies sympathized with American resistance to British imperial policies and aided the Revolutionaries at the outset, but without finally committing themselves to the Revolutionary struggle.

Pancake, John S. *1777: The Year of the Hangman*. University, AL: University of Alabama Press, 1977. Chronicles the fighting of the year 1777, with especially good material on the Saratoga campaign.

———. *This Destructive War: The British Campaign in the Carolinas, 1780–82*. University, AL: University of Alabama Press, 1985. A plainer, but better organized history than Buchanan's of the Revolution in the

Carolinas, concentrating on the fall of Charleston, the debacle at Camden, and the recovery of the rebel fortunes under Greene.

Rakove, Jack. *The Beginnings of National Politics: An Interpretive History of the Continental Congress*. Baltimore: Johns Hopkins University Press, 1979. The classic account of the struggles of the Continental Congress to give political shape to the Revolutionary impulse.

Randall, Willard Sterne. *Benedict Arnold: Patriot and Traitor*. New York: William Morrow and Co., 1990. If it is possible to write a biography of Arnold that makes him believable without also trying to apologize for him, this is it. A full-length treatment.

———. *George Washington: A Life*. New York: Henry Holt, 1997. The best single-volume life of Washington, with ample coverage of Washington's pre-Revolutionary years.

Reich, Jerome R. *British Friends of the American Revolution.*, Armonk, NY: M. E. Sharpe, 1998. A short collection of essays on the principal American sympathizers in Britain and in Parliament.

Reid, Stuart. *British Redcoat, 1740–1793*. London: Osprey, 1996. A volume in the "Men-at-Arms" advanced "Warrior" series, with a highly illuminating discussion of the recruitment, training, and drill of British soldiers in the Revolutionary era.

Royster, Charles. *A Revolutionary People at War: The Continental Army and American Character, 1775–1783*. Chapel Hill: University of North Carolina Press, 1979. A controversial interpretation of the tension between the republican ideals of Revolutionary politics and the professional practice of war as embodied in the Continental soldier.

Schecter, Barnet. *The Battle for New York: The City at the Heart of the American Revolution*. New York: Walker Publishing Company, 2002. A popular history of the role played by New York City in the Revolution, with especially good material on the Battle of Long Island and the struggle for Manhattan.

Selby, John E. *The Revolution in Virginia, 1775–1783*. Williamsburg: Colonial Williamsburg Foundation, 1988. A rapid but very useful survey of Virginia's role in the Revolution, both for the battles fought on its soil and for the political struggle within.

Shy, John. *A People Numerous and Armed: Reflections on the Military Struggle for American Independence*. New York: Oxford University Press, 1976. A collection of Shy's "accidental" essays on the military history of the Revolution.

————. *Toward Lexington: The Role of the British Army in the Coming of the American Revolution*. Princeton, NJ: Princeton University Press, 1965. A shrewd analysis of the command and logistical difficulties faced by the British army in its attempt to police the British North American colonies in the decade before the Revolution.

Silverman, Kenneth. A *Cultural History of the American Revolution*. New York: Crowell, 1976. A vast survey of how the arts—literature, drama, painting, music—were enlisted in the service of the Revolutionary cause, which in turn affected the development of a uniquely American culture.

Smith, Samuel S. *The Battle of Brandywine*. Monmouth Beach, NJ: Philip Freneau Press, 1976. This tall, slim book is the best source on the Battle of Brandywine, with a full record of units involved and maps of the battlefield.

Stephenson, Michael. *Patriot Battles: How the War of Independence Was Fought*. New York: HarperCollins, 2007. A popular history of the soldiers and their battles; the first half of the book is devoted to the weapons and tactics of the British and American armies, while the second half turns to capsule histories of the major battles.

Taafe, Stephen R. *The Philadelphia Campaign, 1777–1778*. Lawrence: University of Kansas Press, 2003. The best single campaign history of the American Revolution, taking in the "big picture" of the battles for Philadelphia from the summer of 1777 until the British evacuation of the rebel capital and the Battle at Monmouth Courthouse.

Taylor, Alan. *American Colonies*. New York: Viking, 2001. A huge survey of the European colonization of North America, with particularly helpful attention to the social and political world of French-speaking, but British-ruled, Canada on the eve of the Revolution.

Thomas, Evan. *John Paul Jones: Sailor, Hero, Father of the American Navy*. New York: Simon & Schuster, 2003. A fine popular history of the first major American naval hero, without attempting to wish away his crude origins or violent, almost psychotic, behavior.

Tower, Charlemagne. *The Marquis de La Fayette in the American Revolution*. Philadelphia: J. B. Lippincott Company, 1895. A vast but still worthwhile compendium of Lafayette's letters and activities in the Revolution.

Trussell, John B. B. *Epic on the Schuylkill: The Valley Forge Encampment, 1777–1778*. Harrisburg: Pennsylvania Historical and Museum Commission, 1974. By a veteran Pennsylvania historian, this thick booklet offers maps, descriptions of units, and the ebb-and-flow of Continental morale during the Valley Forge winter.

van Buskirk, Judith L. *Generous Enemies: Patriots and Loyalists in Revolutionary New York.* Philadelphia: University of Pennsylvania Press, 2002. An unusual interpretation of the divide between rebels and Loyalists in New York that argues that both quietly cooperated across that divide much more than they used it to punish each other.

Volo, James M. *Blue Water Patriots: The American Revolution Afloat.* Westport, CT: Praeger, 2007. A scholarly treatment of the Continental navy, with particularly helpful material on its logistics and command structure.

Walsh, John Evangelist. *The Execution of Major André.* New York: St. Martin's, 2001. A brief popular account of Maj. John André's mission to Benedict Arnold, along with a full retelling of André's capture, trial, and execution; questions the "nobility" of André and defends the integrity of the three militiamen who captured him.

Weintraub, Stanley. *Iron Tears: America's Battle for Freedom, Britain's Quagmire, 1775–1783.* New York: Free Press, 2005. Despite an often-confusing cast of characters and an uncertain narrative line, still the best popular account of British home politics during the Revolution; emphasizes the unpopularity of the American war from the start and the steady decay of support for it in Parliament.

Wolf, Stephanie Grauman. *As Various as Their Land: The Everyday Lives of Eighteenth-Century Americans.* New York: HarperCollins, 1993. A wonderful survey of American social life in the era of the Revolution, examining family life, the creation of domestic space, gender, childhood, the economy, and social networks.

Wood, Gordon. *The Creation of the American Republic, 1776–1787.* Chapel Hill: University of North Carolina Press, 1969. One of the great books on the ideas that ruled the minds of Revolutionary Americans, this time (unlike Bailyn) focusing on the domestic sources of the Revolution's ideology.

Wright, Robert K. *The Continental Army.* Washington, DC: Government Printing Office, 1986. A highly useful analysis of the creation and structure of the Continental army, with particular attention to how Washington developed it out of the New England militia and guided it through two successive reorganizations; the appendices include capsule histories of all Continental regiments.

Wright, Ronald. *Stolen Continents: The Americas through Indian Eyes since 1492*. Boston: Houghton Mifflin, 1992. A passionate brief on behalf of the Indian nations of the American continents, with particularly useful material on the struggle of the Cherokee nation during the Revolution.

Internet Resources

http://etext.lib.virginia.edu/jefferson/. Thomas Jefferson's papers are available electronically through the e-text collection of the University of Virginia.

http://memory.loc.gov/ammem/collections/continental/ and http://www.memory.loc.gov/ammem/amlaw/lwjc.html. These two sites assemble digital images and electronic transcriptions of the Journals of the Continental Congresses and their major publications.

http://memory.loc.gov/ammem/gwhtml/gwhome.html and http://www.rotunda.upress.virginia.edu. These two sites present electronic access to the letters and papers of George Washington. The first is located at the Library of Congress; the second is the digital-access edition of the University of Virginia Press's Papers of George Washington project.

http://www.americanrevolution.com. This is a general-information site on the Revolution, with popular discussions of Revolutionary history, links to other Revolution websites, and a message board.

http://www.britishbattles.com. Although this is a general site devoted to British military history, its web pages offer excellent coverage of the major battles of the Revolution, along with particularly useful maps and uniform illustrations.

http://www.masshist.org/digitaladams/aea/. This site gives digital access to the Adams Family Papers: An Electronic Archive, which includes John Adams's diary, autobiography, and letters.

http://www.nps.gov/revwar/index.html. This site collects into one place access to all the Revolutionary War battlefield sites managed by the National Park Service, with information on the battles, current schedules of events, and directions.

http://www.npg.si.edu/col/age/. This collection offers digitized portraits of the major figures of the Revolution from the collections of the National Portrait Gallery in Washington, DC.

Notes